MY LITTLE
TRAVEL
BLACK BOOKS
COMPILATION

The Ultimate Guide to Travel Hacks to show you how to afford to travel when you want to and where you want to without breaking the bank.

CHRISTINA SANDERS
© 2018

MY LITTLE TRAVEL BLACK BOOKS
Copyright © 2018 by (Brilliant! Wanderer)

For permission requests, write to the publisher, addressed "Attention: My Little Travel Black Books Permissions Request," at the email address below:

brilliantwanderer@gmail.com

ISBN (978-0-578-47927-9)

Printed in USA

Dedication

Dear Lord,

No matter what it looks like...if not for your grace...
Thank You most of all for loving me unconditionally.

Since thou wast precious in my sight,
thou hast been honourable, and I have loved thee – Isaiah 43:4

Love…
- More than a conqueror!

In Loving Memory of my beautiful mother Estelle Sanders
You are irreplaceable, even in your earthly absence
You were the gift that I couldn't have prayed the perfect prayer for
You were chosen just for me
I can only hope that I enhance the legacy you left behind
You ran well Mama and passed the baton on to me
I'm gonna finish strong, just like you did!

~~Eternally grateful ~ ~
Love You Forever,
"Chris"

My precious cousin
DaShaur Larjuan Tamar Allen
You were the little sister I never had
but my favorite little cousin ever
I miss you...
Love you always baby girl
1986 - Forever

Love,
Chris

Contents

Foreword

My Little Travel Black Book

The Ultimate Guide to Travel Hacks to show you how to afford to travel when you want to and where you want to without breaking the bank.

The Purpose of this Guide: This guide is not only to encourage you to travel but to live and enjoy your life NOW! To expose your children to new cultures...To motivate you to take BIG risks in order to have and experience the life that you were destined to live: One city, state, country, continent, goal, or dream at a time.

Disclaimer: This is based on my own research and some personal experiences. The information that I am sharing with you does not guarantee lower-cost travel, but it will give you the strategies to help save you money in various ways that either you may or may not have known about. They do require some work in order to get the best deals possible, but if you are willing to put the work in then it will be worth your every effort.

Who is this guide for? Couples, Solo, Digital Nomads, Families, Groups, Students, Location Independent Entrepreneurs...anyone who wants to travel and save money while you're at it!

In this guide you will learn the following:

* Oh! Oh! Oh! The many places you can go!!!

* 3 most affordable ways to travel

* 3 ways to save on airfare

* Best way to plan your dream trip

* What the world is a stopover?

* How to make the most of your time when you're stuck at the airport

* Alternatives to traditional hotels

* 3 tips for using Airbnb effectively

* How to not look like a tourist and blend in with the locals

* How to get the guts to solo travel

* Where and How to find the best places to eat

* Using the power of Social Media to find the best travel deals

* Unconventional car rental service

Let's Go!

Think you can't afford to travel? Think again!

Here are some common excuses for not traveling:

Excuse #1: Traveling is too expensive. I need a lot of money to do so.

Excuse #2: I don't have anyone to travel with and I'm too scared to travel by myself

Excuse #3: I don't have enough time to travel

Excuse #4: One day I will...

Excuse #5: I can't speak or understand a different language

I am going to show you ways that travel can be a commonplace in your life as well as encourage you that there are no valid excuses. It can be done.

I was about 2 years old and my mom had taken me on my first plane trip to Los Angeles to visit our family. I vaguely remember this trip, but I do recall feeling like a little Shirley Temple, all dressed up in my little sailor dress, sheepishly parading down the airplane isle as the flight attendants wanted to show me off to the other passengers. If I would have had it in me back then, I probably would have broken out with the one of her most notable songs "*On the Good Ship Lollipop*". Anyway, during this trip, was when I received my first "wings" pin, thanks to American Airlines. I had unknowingly gained my wings to travel. My mom sat on the aisle seat, I was in the middle, and there was some nice gentleman sitting next to the window. He had asked my mom if he could hold me for a minute so that I could look out the window. She cautiously allowed him to do so. On to LA we went and what a treat it was.

We went to Disneyland and all. One of my uncle's wanted to take me out into the ocean, my mom said that we got swept out a bit too far and some scuba divers had to rescue us. I don't remember much of that trip, only through some pictures that I still have. I guess my mom was right because in a picture there were two men dressed in black scuba diving suits posing as I'm looking a bit confused with my little hand in my mouth, wondering what I should do with my once cute and fluffy white dress and baby blue sweater and my freshly parted pigtails, now drenched with ocean water.

From there, I remember the many road trips back and forth to my mom's hometown of Ft. Smith, Arkansas and had always enjoyed the feeling of going somewhere. My mom always made our road trips a learning lesson, so basically whatever I was learning in school at that time, she'd try to quiz me about it on the road. Especially if we'd pass a sign, she'd ask me to read it or point out what a particular point of interest was and have me explain to her what it stood for. I still remember the irrigation systems that we would pass and my mom would ask me what it was. I was learning about that in 4th grade, I think. It's deeply embedded in my memory and hopefully one day I will be able to share those lessons with my family.

I'm grateful that my mother desired to expose me to new places. She would allow me to travel with my high school band and church groups to different states and cities. I've heard of many stories in which people have never been on an airplane let alone out of their own hometown or state, so I'm very grateful for the opportunities I've been given.

Exposure is a necessary way of life. Leaving your surroundings and being exposed to other cultures, new people, and new experiences allows one to expand their own way of thinking and realize that there is so much more out in the world to offer than the same streets and highways that they often pass on a daily basis.

The Atlas and the Globe

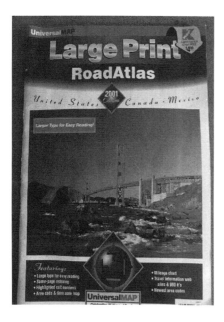

One of my favorite past times as a child was looking through my mom's atlas. I honestly cannot tell you why but I knew there was a world out there far beyond my home state of Oklahoma. Even though I had visited several states with my mom, church or school, there were so many other places that I had always heard about and wanted to learn more of. So, my true travel journey started in my imagination. I could spend countless hours studying a state and being fascinated by all the details including the interstates and roads, rivers, main cities and beyond.

Same with the globe. I had always admired the globe that my granny had at her house. It was something that was in the family and when my mom and I would visit, I would always play around with the globe, thinking to myself" One *day I am going to see these places"*. That globe meant so much to me. In fact, my Aunt Laura doesn't know this but I happened to be visiting one weekend from college and she was holding a garage sale. I remember looking at the globe and was a little sad as this sparked so many childhood memories. Little did she know how much it meant to me, she offered to give it to me and I still have it to this day. Call me sentimental, I am. However, I really believe that travel has always been in my blood. Like many of you, I haven't traveled the globe but desire to do so one city, state, country, and continent at a time.

How I broke the cycle of holding myself back from living life

A little background about how I started my travel journey. Back in 2002, I moved back to my hometown and after a year of being home, I realized that I needed a change of scenery. That's what keeps me motivated, especially after living in and visiting larger cities that had a bit more to offer. I remember it was about a week out and I was looking at a map for places that I had never had been to and decided to go to New York City. It was totally on a whim! At the time, my budget was limited and I was looking for an affordable way to make this dream happen. I searched high and low, looked at airplane tickets and got a little bit discouraged because I had waited until the last minute, so ticket prices were unbearably high, especially flying from my neck of the woods. I decided to try Amtrak. Sure, it was going to be a longer journey, but I was able to see parts of the country as well as meet interesting people along my journey that I would have never seen or met had I not taken this path. Plus, as the trip went on, I realized that my fear of "going solo" was slowly dissipating.

From there, I booked with Amtrak and then the next task was to find a place to stay. I had always heard that New York City with a very expensive place to visit let alone trying to find a decent place to lodge without breaking the bank. So, I decided to try an unconventional method. I decided to search through Craigslist. Yes, I said Craigslist! This was before the days of Airbnb and other alternative lodging startups were born. Craigslist was a bit safer than it is today. I can't say I would try that method now but it worked for me then and I don't regret it one bit.

I looked day in and day out and there were options that caught my interest but I was a little leery. What if these people are crazy? What if I get there and this post was fake and I'm stuck in this big city all by myself? Well, trust me, I had questions but in the back of my mind, but with every question, I had a backup plan. Trust me!

It wasn't until this Bed and Breakfast host had messaged me personally and asked me if I was still looking for a place to stay. I was a little taken back that she knew that I was looking but I think that I had placed a post of 'in search of' and then deleted it a day or two later. I inquired a bit more as to what she had to offer and negotiated on that offer. Remember, I had a tight budget and it worked for her because she just needed to find someone to fill the open spot so that she was able to meet her weekly occupancy goal. Much to my surprise, I found out that she had a very nice Brownstone in Brooklyn in which she hosted several travelers at a time. I performed extensive background research and finally made peace with my decision. She had given me her information so that we could talk directly by phone and she reached out to me all the way until it was time for me to board the train and start my journey. It was the best decision I could have ever made for my first real solo trip. I stayed in New York City for about seven days and paid in under $500 for the whole trip excluding my meals, entertainment, and some small souvenirs. You might be thinking what in the world could you get in New York for $500 but let me tell you, it is possible! That's when I made up my mind that I would do the proper research before making final plans on a trip, getaway, or vacation. I realized that it's not as hard as we think it is but it does take a little time and proper planning to make it all happen.

Even though I've done some extensive research, the purpose of this guide book is to help you cut to the chase and have the necessary resources at hand to help you save time, money, as well as save you from the excuses that you cannot do it.

How to make the most out of a trip

I get it. You're reading this for some quick answers as to how to get the best bang for your buck. Take this scenario: Do you have a big trip that you are planning or maybe you are going to a large city or somewhere near one? Maybe you decided to take a cruise from a port with major surrounding cities, I bet you are already catching on! Well, if you plan it out properly you can take one trip and make multiple trips within it.

A few years ago, I was headed the Virgin Islands or the Bahamas, sorry it was a while back so I think I might be mixing up my story a little (please forgive me - smile -), but wherever I was going I had to fly into of Miami. In fact, when I booked my flight, I specifically chose to fly into Miami and I looked to see how long of a layover I could get before I flew out or back into Florida. I intentionally chose a 5-hour layover in Miami. Guess what I did? You already know...I figured out a way to actually tour Miami Beach and get back to the airport in time. I mean, why not?

I figured an Uber would be quite expensive and the whole idea was to explore as much as possible while saving money in the process. Google and travel groups can be your best friend, trust me. I googled buses from MIA to South Beach and #BINGO, I was able to find that I could do just like that for pennies on the dollar. They actually have kiosks in the airport for you to purchase bus tickets and there was someone there that was able to give me the right instructions so that my spontaneous travel plans would go smoothly.

You are probably thinking, what about your luggage? Well, in some airports, they have lockers and you pay a little bit to lock your luggage up for a few hours and that's exactly what I did. I mean really, what would I look like walking down South Beach while everyone is in bikinis and trunks and I am fully dressed with my full-sized luggage. Those wheels don't always work right anyway, you start out rolling and then somehow those wheels get off track and your bag goes haywire, rocking back and forth and stuff. Nope, that's not cute at all!

Anyway, I locked my bags up, put my messenger bag over my shoulder and off I went. Oh yeah and I changed into some cute clothing, after all, I was in Miami baby!!! That was the first time I visited Miami and it was an awesome experience. I had lunch and walked around South Beach, just exploring to my heart's content. I kept my eye on the time and allotted myself more than an hour or so to get back to the airport. Even though it was about a 2.5-hour tour, I was completely satisfied.

I tried this technique another time and this was I believe the first time I had mapped out such a trip, but I had wanted to visit Washington DC but I also had family in the Norfolk/Virginia Beach area and since I was out that way, I calculated my timing to determine how I could cover all these points. One of my good friends, Monica, often told me about how beautiful Virginia Beach was so I had to see it for myself.

In fact, I pulled up a map (Google Maps) of the general areas that I wanted to visit and laid out my plan. I entered in 'Washington DC to Virginia Beach' and it returned a route and how long it would take. It was about 3.5 hours and for me, that drive is nothing. I could have driven straight down the suggested path, but I wanted to take a more scenic route, so I decided to go through Maryland in order to take the Chesapeake Bay Bridge Tunnel. It was a little out of the way, but it was truly an adventure. Google it!!! Now a lot of people talk about it being scary because it's about a 20-minute scenic view of the Atlantic Ocean. You are driving over nothing but water for 20 minutes or so. It was one of the most beautiful experiences ever and it took me straight into Norfolk/Virginia Beach area.

Don't be afraid to travel off the beaten path. Be safe, but try something different. Explore it. When you do, you will have created some awesome memories and experiences that will be worth every dime you spend on your trip.

Here's some tips to make the most out of your next trip:

- Plan ahead and map out your exploration
- Flexibility is key
- Book a flight with a long layover in or near a big city or somewhere you've always wanted to visit

- Check local bus schedules or Uber costs (even see how much you can get done by walking - pick a city that walking is the norm)

- Have fun

Popular cities to explore on foot

While it would be quite a journey to explore a whole city by walking, some would probably opt out on that one, but there are cities that have areas in which you can see and do a lot on foot.

1. New York City

2. Chicago

3. Las Vegas

4. Miami

5. San Antonio

6. Washington, DC

7. Philadelphia

8. Boston

9. Oakland, CA

10. Minneapolis

7 Travel Tips that you can use to get organized

1. Create a separate Gmail account specifically for travel and set up price alerts

2. Sign up for airline emails – go to carrier websites like Delta.com, AA.com, Southwestairlines.com, etc., and sign up for their email – Often times they offer deals from your specified location but they are limited time offers and change weekly

3. Download Mobile apps or create browser bookmarks for your travel hacks (create shareable bookmarks)

4. Create a Twitter list and activate notifications

5. Sign up for Facebook Travel Groups

6. Set a travel goal - pick a destination, set a date, and start planning

7. Setup a Google Voice phone number so that you can send all offers to voicemail

My Favorite Apps

I love mobile apps and the power that technology enables us to have instant access to resources at the tap of our fingers. My phone is loaded with all the travel apps that I use at any given time. Throughout this book, I've tried to give more details of how they work but I wanted to share with you my personal collection. Yes, these are all loaded on my phone!

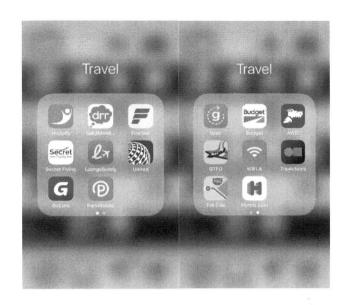

Websites (and apps) to find the best travel deals:

Skyscanner - www.skyscanner.com - Skyscanner is a leading global travel search site, a place where people are inspired to plan and book direct from millions of travel options at the best prices.

Airfare Watchdog - www.airfarewatchdog.com - Airfare deals, cheap flights, & money-saving tips from our experts. Track prices with our fare watcher alerts!

Secret Flying - www.secretflying.com - Super cheap flight deals that you have to be ready to grab when you see them. You snooze, you lose!

Hotel Tonight - www.hoteltonight.com - Find last minute hotel deals

Hopper - www.hopper.com - Hopper analyzes billions of prices daily to predict how prices will change, and tells you whether to buy or wait. Save up to 40% on your next flight.

Kayak - www.kayak.com - KAYAK is a travel search aggregator that explores hundreds of travel sites at once to find the information you need to make the right decisions on flights, hotels & rental cars.

Hipmunk - www.hipmunk.com - Hipmunk brings in travel options ranging from commercial flights to trains to charter flights and accommodations ranging from large hotels to home and apartments rentals through Airbnb and Homeaway.

GTFO! - www.gtfoflights.com - Get The Flight Out mailing list of crazy flight deals, most up to 80% off, delivered to your inbox 2-3 times per week.

BookingBuddy - www.bookingbuddy.com - Travel search engine.

Expedia - www.expedia.com - One of the most popular travel search sites offering exclusive deals, travel packages, and reviews.

Kiwi - kiwi.com - Find discounts on flights, hotels, trains, and car services.

Apple Vacations - www.applevacations.com - Offers all-inclusive travel packages and payment plans.

Travel Zoo - www.travelzoo.com - A mailing list and website that publishes offers from more than 2,000 travel, entertainment and local companies. Travelzoo's deal experts review offers to find the best deals and confirm their true value. You can find some great travel packages that include flight and hotel for various trip lengths.

The Flight Deal - https://www.theflightdeal.com - Publishes deals by flight per mile of 6 cents or less per mile. For example, they revealed a flight from Dallas, Texas to Maui, Hawaii for $257 roundtrip. They break down the steps to achieve this deal but you must be flexible. It's worth checking out.

The Fare Deal - www.faredealalert.com - Specializing in curated travel deals from Atlanta, Charlotte, Denver, Detroit, Houston, Kansas City, Las Vegas, Minneapolis, Orlando, and San Diego.

Kayak Explore - www.kayak.com/explore - Is an extension from the kayak.com website but explore let's you search for destinations within your suggested budget. In the example below, I selected a budget of $500 with any stops from Oklahoma City. I decided to choose Montreal, Canada between September 1st and September 4th. It returned a roundtrip fare for $276 for an extended Labor Day Weekend. By clicking on the fare, you can see the breakdown of the flight costs.

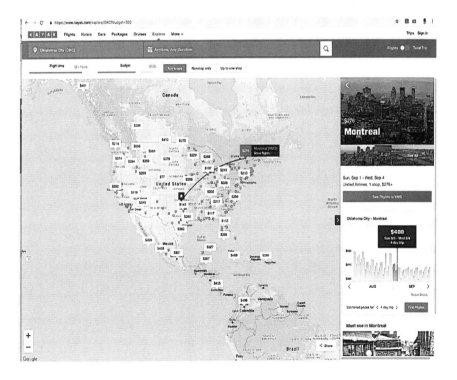

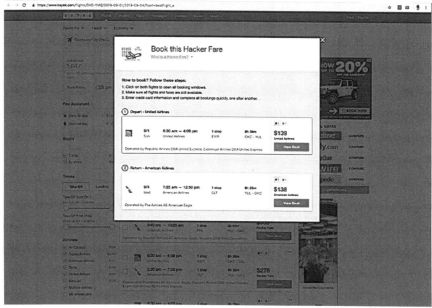

Wander - www.wander.am - Wander is another site that you can enter your desired destination and budget and it will offer suggestions. I used San Antonio as the departure city and set a travel budget of up to $1200 (for flight and hotel) and a plethora of options returned:

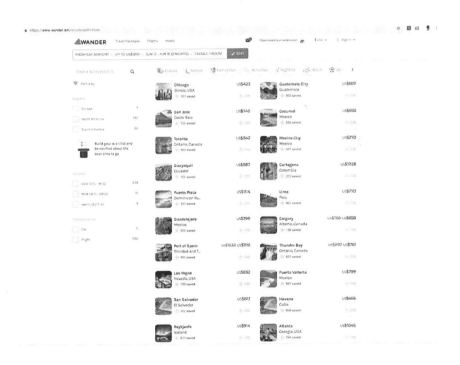

Trip Planning:
TripIt - www.tripit.com

Best Reviews and Recommendations:
TripAdvisor - www.tripadvisor.com –
Hotels and services reviews based on customer/traveler
experiences
Yelp - www.yelp.com - Restaurants and business reviews
Oyster - www.oyster.com - Hotel reviews

Hotel Alternatives:
Airbnb - www.airbnb.com
VRBO - www.vrbo.com - Vacation Rental by Owner

Transportation Services:
Uber - www.uber.com
TURO - www.turo.com
SilverCar - www.silvercar.com
Rail Europe - www.raileurope.com

Your favorite airline carrier app
American Airlines - www.aa.com
Southwest Airlines - www.southwest.com
Delta Airlines - www.delta.com
United Airlines - www.united.com
Frontier Airlines - www.flyfrontier.com
Ethiad Airways - www.ethiad.com
British Airways - www.britishairways.com

Food Delivery Services:
DoorDash - www.doordash.com
UberEats - www.ubereats.com
Grab - www.grabapp.com - Skip the lines while at the airport

Airport Lounges:
Lounge Buddy - www.loungebuddy.com
Lounge Pass - www.loungepass.com
Priority Pass - www.prioritypass.com

Specialty sites (blogs and more):
Studentfares - www.studentfares.com
Flyertalk - www.flyertalk.com
Jetsetter - www.jetsetter.com
Boarding Area - www.boardingarea.com
Hotels by Day - www.hotelsbyday.com
Cruise Critic - https://www.cruisecritic.com/
Cruise Line - https://cruiseline.com/
Triposo - www.triposo.com

Things to do:
Peek - peek.com – Discover and book exciting things to do for your trip.

Miscellaneous:

Digit Savings - https://digit.co - Digit analyzes your spending and automatically saves the perfect amount every day, so you don't have to ... Share what you're saving for and Digit does the rest.

GateGuru is another app that helps organize your trip's itinerary by automatically arranging your forwarded email confirmation into one schedule. Besides just creating an easy to read itinerary, GateGuru also breaks down the airports where you will be departing and arriving. It lets you know where the closest ATM is, where you can find free Wi-Fi, and which restaurants are closest to your terminal.

City Maps 2 Go:
Download for iOS:
https://itunes.apple.com/at/app/citymaps2go-reisekarte/id408866084

Download for Google Play:
https://play.google.com/store/apps/details?id=com.ulmon.android.citymaps2go&hl=de_AT (search Google for City Maps 2 Go)

Student Universe - www.studentuniverse.com - Website loaded with student fare travel deals

Shipmate - https://shipmateapp.com/ - Mobile app covering a multitude of cruise itineraries from popular cruise lines. You can track cruises, see who you're sailing with, view deck plans, review and traveler photos.

Funjet - www.funjet.com – Website of various travel packages and deals to all-inclusive resorts.

Rocket Miles - https://www.rocketmiles.com - will help you earn points toward companion passes, etc

Language translation apps
iTranslate - https://www.itranslate.com/
Trip Lingo - http://triplingo.com/
Google Translate - https://translate.google.com/

Currency converter apps
XE - https://www.xe.com
Currency App - http://currencyapp.com/
Google Search: Currency Converter

Email Deals

Some of the best deals come through being on certain email lists. While most lists offer free subscriptions, they also have a paid subscription as well. The yearly subscriptions are often pretty low for around $20 to $40. If you don't think you will be using it much, just stay on the free plan. To get added to the email list, you simply enter your email address and departure city and as a subscriber you will receive a daily or weekly email spelling out the best flights. So, you won't miss these deals or they won't get lost within the array of your other emails, you can create a separate email account just for travel. This helps you to keep things organized.

If you don't see an offer from your city, remember to search for the next city closest to you. If it's a great deal then it will be worth the drive. Keep in mind the the deals are often time sensitive so catch them while you can.

Hitlist - (www.hitlist.com) - sends you travel deals within one to two weeks of the email distribution date.

Scott's Cheap Flights - www.scottscheapflights.com - The story of how Scott's Cheap Flights started is simply amazing. Scott Keyes turned his hobby of finding cheap plane tickets into a 7 figure business and email list. Only a short few years ago, Scott Keyes had come across a deal from NYC to Milan for about $130 roundtrip. He was so floored by his findings, he started spreading the word and people hooked on thus Scott's Cheap Flights was born.

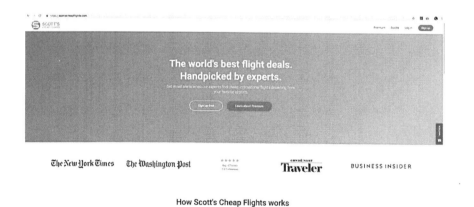

Did you mean: scott's cheap flights

	Scott's Cheap Fligh.	Inbox	Toronto ~ $200s (RT, bags extra, some NYE avail) Nov - Sep - all the cheap flight alerts [if mso]> Get ALL the deals All about this widespread deal to Toronto. Some routes even include	10/14/18
	Scott's Cheap Fligh.	Inbox	Beijing or Shanghai ~ $300s-$500s (RT, no bag fees) Nov - May - all the cheap flight alerts. [if mso]> Get ALL the deals Beijing or Shanghai because having options is never the worst	10/12/18
	Scott's Cheap Fligh.	Inbox	widespread Europe sale ~ $400s/$500s (RT, no bag fees) Nov - May - all the cheap flight alerts [if mso]> Get ALL the deals Deals > Sleep. Write not weird. Although not every origin	10/12/18
	Scott's Cheap Fligh.	Inbox	Middle East ~ $500s/low-$600s (RT, no bag fees) Nov - May - all the cheap flight alerts [if mso]> Get ALL the deals This deal doesn't come around as often anymore. excited when	10/11/18
	Scott's Cheap Fligh.	Inbox	*rare* Africa ~ $500s/$600s (RT, no bag fees) Nov - May - all the cheap flight alerts [if mso]> Get ALL the deals By far one of the largest Africa deals that we've seen, with	10/11/18
	Scott's Cheap Fligh.	Inbox	*more cities added* Europe ~ $300s/$400s (RT, bags extra) Nov - May - all the cheap flight alerts [if mso]> Get ALL the deals Europe has been popping up all over the place, all about it. Not	10/10/18
	Scott's Cheap Fligh.	Inbox	*price drop* Tokyo ~ $505 (RT, no bag fees) Oct - Dec - all the cheap flight alerts. [if mso]> Get ALL the deals Sweet price drops to Tokyo :-) No bag fees, etc. Travel tip. If you	10/9/18
	Scott's Cheap Fligh.	Inbox	Barcelona or Madrid ~ $300s (RT, bags extra) Nov - May - all the cheap flight alerts [if mso]> Get ALL the deals Spain vs the $300s is a quality way to start the day. These routes	10/9/18
	Scott's Cheap Fligh.	Inbox	EUROPE SALE ~ $300s/$400s (RT, no bag fees) Sep - Dec - all the cheap flight alerts [if mso]> Get ALL the deals http://scottscheapflights emlink1.com/lt.php?s=283d3e52c5e6Ac06tfa4dcbbb467ac0b9&...	5/18/18
	Scott's Cheap Fligh.	Inbox	Mexico City ~ $200s/$300s (RT, bags extra) May - Mar - all the cheap flight alerts [if mso]> Get ALL the deals Mexico City. An SCF favorite. A checked bag will cost about $25	5/11/18
	Scott's Cheap Fligh.	Inbox	Lima ~ $400s (RT, no bag fees) May - Jun / Aug - Mar - all the cheap flight alerts [if mso]> Get ALL the deals Solid fares to Peru :-) No bag fees, etc. All prices roundtrip.	4/26/18
	Scott's Cheap Fligh.	Inbox	Antigua ~ $515 (RT, bags extra) Aug - Feb - all the cheap flight alerts [if mso]> Get ALL the deals Antigua is typically one of the more expensive Caribbean islands	4/7/18

Dollar Flight Club - www.dollarflightclub.com - *Dollar Flight Club* is an email subscription service that helps hundreds of thousands of people save an outrageous amount of money on airfare. Subscribers save over $500 USD per international ticket on average.

Take a look at some of the emails that I receive from them. When you select an option from their email, it will take you to the dashboard with the current/past deals. After you pick one of the deals, it will offer suggested flight dates in order to obtain the price.

Travel Zoo - www.travelzoo.com - Travel deals on hotels, flights, vacation packages, cruises and local & entertainment deals too.

Travel Zoo website

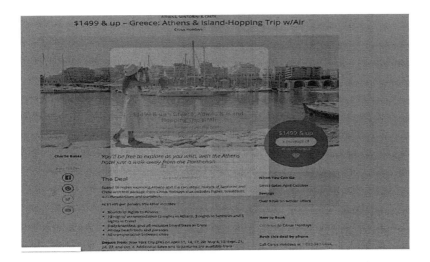

Travel Zoo email – You can see that they offer a mixture of travel deals that will hopefully spark some ideas.

37

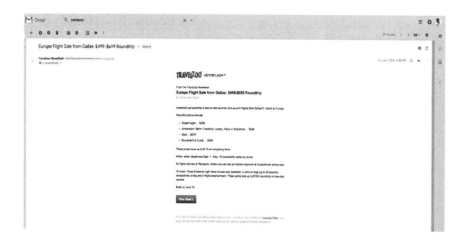

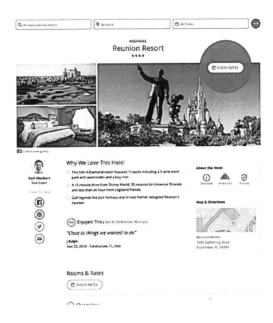

Travel Cheaters - https://www.travelcheaters.com/ - all the flights are roundtrip and updated daily. You have the option to search their site or either review their emails. On their website, it will display the list of departure states which you can select or deselect. Just find your state or the one closest to you as an alternative and it will populate all the deals for that day. They also show deals for premium economy to business class flights.

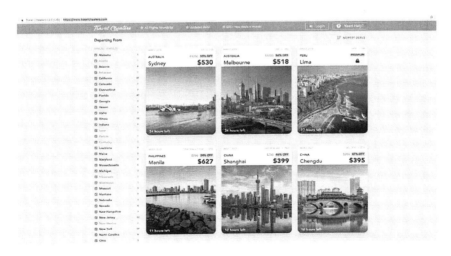

Hitlist - www.hitlist.com - Hitlist locates the cheapest flights from your local airport to worldwide destinations by searching millions of flight prices in a matter of a few seconds.

Jetsetter - www.jetsetter.com - offers premium insider deals and flash sales on their site and through their email list which are a step above the rest.

Error Fares

Error Fares: - Error fares that you can get great deals at a steal. Are these legitimate? Yes, but not guaranteed. It is up to the airline partner to determine if they will eat up the costs or decline the transaction. If they decide to approve it, you've got a great deal in your hands. Travel on!

One known resource for identifying error fares is **Secret Flying** - Secretflying.com is a service that reveals awesome travel deals based on airline fare mistakes which are posted on Twitter, Facebook, IG, Email, and a Mobile App. You have to grab them while you can because there is a short window of opportunity so monitoring Twitter or Instagram are the two most effective sources to catch the deals. If you have some money to spare and want great deals then check one of the Secret Flying promotions out.

Here are some sample flight deals that I think you will be wowed by:

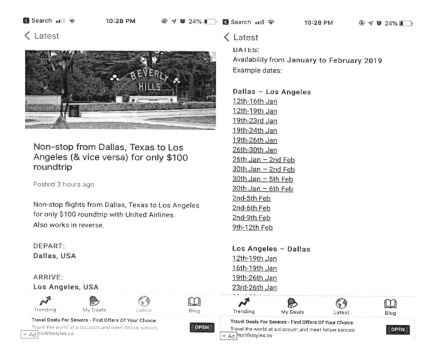

Left screen:

Search .ıl 🛜   10:28 PM   @ ⊿ 🔋 24% ▮

< Latest

Non-stop from Dallas, Texas to Los Angeles (& vice versa) for only $100 roundtrip

Posted 3 hours ago

Non-stop flights from Dallas, Texas to Los Angeles for only $100 roundtrip with United Airlines. Also works in reverse.

DEPART:
Dallas, USA

ARRIVE:
Los Angeles, USA

Trending   My Deals   Latest   Blog

Right screen:

Search .ıl 🛜   10:28 PM   @ ⊿ 🔋 24% ▮

< Latest

DATES:
Availability from **January to February 2019**
Example dates:

Dallas – Los Angeles
12th-16th Jan
12th-19th Jan
19th-23rd Jan
19th-24th Jan
19th-26th Jan
26th-30th Jan
26th Jan – 2nd Feb
30th Jan – 2nd Feb
30th Jan – 5th Feb
30th Jan – 6th Feb
2nd-5th Feb
2nd-6th Feb
2nd-9th Feb
9th-12th Feb

Los Angeles – Dallas
12th-19th Jan
16th-19th Jan
19th-26th Jan
23rd-26th Jan

Trending   My Deals   Latest   Blog

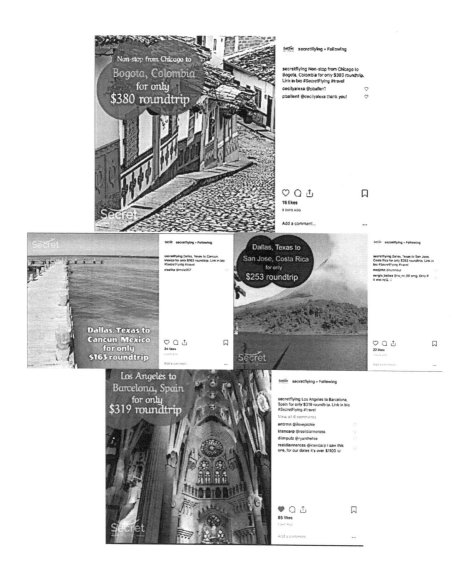

Don't have an idea of where you want to go? Do you have a set travel budget that you would like to stick to? There are actual websites and apps that will allow you to enter in a budget and estimated date range to get an idea of the various destinations that you can go that are within your budget. These are excellent resources to not only study and plan your dream vacation but also expand your mind to the endless possibilities that you hadn't even thought of. I am going to share with you 3 resources that will help you do just that.

Wherefor (www.wherefor.com) is a website that will allow you to enter a budget amount for both airfare and hotel and it will return a map of results highlighting all the places you can go for your set budget. The bonus to this feature is that it will allow you to select the bundled price or select the airfare or hotel rate individually.

45

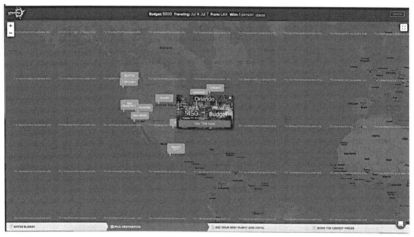

In the example from the search from Los Angeles within my allotted budget, I selected to Orlando from the map. If you notice below, the budget is broken down to both hotel and airfare. You can choose from here to just either book the hotel by itself or the flight by itself. In this case, I would probably select the flight as this a low price, especially to spend the 4th of July week in Florida. It is a red eye from, but for the price, it's worth it! What do you think? Isn't that awesome? Go try it out now! (www.wherefor.com)

Whichbudget (www.whichbudget.com) is a search aggregator that functions very similar to wherefor.com but allows you to perform an open search and it will return the cheapest flights.

Tip: *If you don't have a destination in mind, typical search tools will allow you to enter the word "Anywhere" or "Everywhere" in the Destination/To field and it will return any results available.*

In the example below, I searched for any roundtrip flights leaving from Dallas, Texas to "Anywhere" with no specified date range. When you leave this as an open search, this is how you are able to catch the deals in real time.

The results are listed in the results window on the right-hand side. It lists the price (in bold), beneath that is the date of travel and the destinations are listed underneath the city of departure along with the carrier. See how easy this is? You grab a couple of these low-cost deals and you will be traveling in no time, all the time.

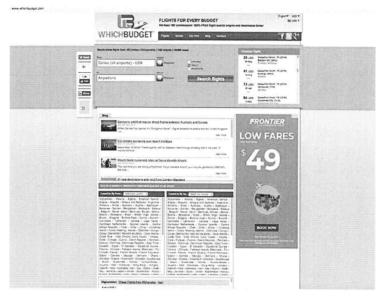

SkyScanner (www.skyscanner.net) is very similar to the other two listed above but this one is also a mobile app. For training purposes, I am showing you the actual site. Note: If you notice the blue pop-up box option that notifies that you can use the search entry 'Everywhere' for more flexible destination options. What I like about Skyscanner's interface is a bit cleaner with minimal ads on the site so that you can focus on choosing a trip. This site or mobile app will allow you to also search for Hotels and Car Rentals.

I entered "Everywhere" and this is a sample of the results. Their search results are organized in such a way that it will give you starting prices based on the country so you can have a wide variety of options to choose from. This also helps you to think outside the box a bit, especially if you really don't have an idea of where to go within a reasonable budget.

skyscanner

✈ Flights   **🛏 Hotels**   **🚗 Car Rental**

From	To	Depart	Return
Dallas (DFWA)	Everywhere	Cheapest mo...	Cheapest mo...

Non-stop flights only

Estimated lowest prices only. Found in the last 15 days.

United States	from $39	⌄
Mexico	from $125	⌄
Canada	from $175	⌄
El Salvador	from $204	⌄
Guatemala	from $224	⌄
Peru	from $226	⌄
Costa Rica	from $232	⌄
Colombia	from $234	⌄
Cuba	from $239	⌄
Puerto Rico	from $256	⌄
US Virgin Islands	from $294	⌄
Dominican Republic	from $295	⌄

50

You can also set up a price alert to be notified as the prices go down.

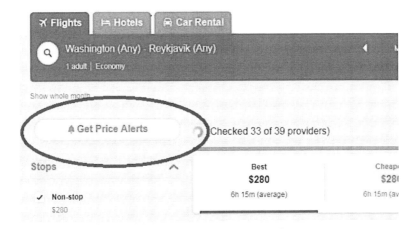

They also have *Daily Flight Deals* that are worth checking out.

Top Daily Flight Deals

Departure City	Destination	Round-Trip Fare
Boston	Denver	$236
Boston	San Francisco	$214
Chicago	Las Vegas	$98
Chicago	Puerto Vallarta	$327
Los Angeles	New York City	$197
Los Angeles	Toronto	$284
Miami	Cancun	$198
Miami	Honolulu	$625
New York City	Orlando	$95
New York City	Washington, DC	$156

Take a weekend trip

Pack your bags; get in your car, and go! Just like that. A few years back, I decided to take a trip to St. Louis to eat at the --- acclaimed Sweetie Pies, with Oprah's stamp of approval. In mapping out my course, I decided to loop around through Memphis, Little Rock, and back home. I did this over Memorial Day weekend. 1400 miles all by myself and I enjoyed the journey. Along the way, I made stops at places like the World's Largest Souvenir Shop, George Washington Carver's memorial center, Martin Luther King/Lorraine Hotel.

Unbeknownst to me, I found that Washington University in St. Louis had an on-campus hotel, which provided first class service that literally blew my mind. Breakfast was included. The campus was very beautiful and the whole experience was much more than I could have ever asked for.

Jump on a cruise

Why a cruise? Because once you've figured out how to get to the cruise port, either by plane, train, or automobile, once you get on the cruise ship itself, your life will be transformed into an instant vacation wonderland full of food, entertainment, and fun.

So, aren't cruises expensive? The answer to this is yes and no, but again you have to know when and where to look. Maybe you have some time coming up and decide to take a cruise at the last minute. The best part about taking a last-minute cruise is you can find phenomenal last-minute specials offering low, low rates because the cruise line wants to fill their vacant cabins.

To find the best last minute cruise offerings, you can go to the cruise line website itself or go the sites like www.lastminutecruises.com www.cruisedeals.com, www.vacationstogo.com . You can even score a cruise for as low as $179 but you have to be flexible in your travel dates or book early enough in order to grab those deals.

Signing up with forums like www.cruisecritic.com or www.cruiseline.com will definitely give you insights from other travelers, from experienced to first time cruisers. You can find out where to go, what to do, what not to do, etc. along with various tips on how to pack. Careful research an interaction is key!

Are you a little scared and skeptical about taking a cruise? Don't hold back. You can explore the world, in fine fashion this way.

Explore by train

As mentioned, a bit earlier, this is what ignited the travel bug in me. I must say, you must have the patience of Job to be able to take a train trip because in the USA it is a lot of stopping and starting. You can also experience some layovers by this mode of transportation as well but taking a train trip can be one of the most adventurous experiences that you will ever have in your life. You will be able to see parts of the countryside that you've never seen before and you don't have to do it driving yourself. Some of the most beautiful and relaxing rides is taking a train down the coastline as well as through the Rockies and the likes. Amtrak is one of the most popular train lines in North America, but then there is the Rocky Mountaineer, that goes through the Canadian Rockies, Euro rail that travels through various countries in Europe, as well as the most coveted train ride, The Orient Express??? The Venice Simplon-Orient Express, but you have various options as you travel outside the United States.

8 Ways to Save on Airfare

1.   *Be flexible with your travel dates* - this is one of the best tips out there. If you are not set on a time period to travel, this might be a pivotal move to earn the greatest savings. Instead of departing on a Thursday or Friday, consider traveling on a Tuesday or Wednesday.

2.   *Start looking and booking early* - Booking at least 3 months ahead can render

3.   *Use a travel map to determine the best times to travel*

4.   *Clear your browser cookies* – if you keep refreshing your browser, you will notice that the price changes this is because it is based on the "demand". In essence, pinging the website multiple times thinking the price will change or even revisiting it within a few days of the first search will increase the demand effect.

5.   *Use travel apps* - There right at your fingertips and you can often capture some of the best deals on the fly. Refer to my personal travel app selections later on in this book.

6.   *Carry on your carry-on* - Depending on the length of your trip, you could probably use smart packing techniques to fill your carry-on bag and take it with you on the plane. This can cut your expenses by at least $25. It may not sound like much but round trip that's $50 and its $50 more in your bank account or you can use toward spending money.

7.   *Fly out of another airport* - If you are closer to another airport that you can drive to for answers, you might want to consider it because your flights might be cheaper.

8.   *Buy a one-way ticket.* Consider purchasing one-way tickets at separate times. Oftentimes, you can find better deals by splitting your airfare in half.

Stuck at the airport for a long period of time?

Get out, grab an Uber and go site seeing! Depending on how fast I am trying to reach my destination, I might purposely pick a route through a city that I like or have never been to and if it is a rather lengthy layover, over 3 hours then out of the airport I go and on to seeing what I can see. You might be asking, what about your luggage? If I only have a carry on, I just make sure that it is either a bag with rollers or a backpack (with rollers). Some airports have baggage storage places that you can check your bags in while you roam through the airport or through a city. Prices typically start at $10 per bag.

Prior to a trip, I make sure that I have laid out a plan of where I'd like to go, determine a place to grab something good to eat (I use Yelp to find a place in close proximity with the best reviews), and then on to my exploration. Most major airports are in a location in which you can get to a shopping center or other major points of interest and still have time to spare to get back to the airport, go through the security checkpoints, and on to your gate. It may be a bit too much for some, but this guide is about enjoying life. Come on, live a little!

Using Airport Lounges without being a First-Class member

The coveted airport lounges, where flyers can relax, grab a drink or ors d'oeuvres, or just kick back relax, enjoy free Wi-Fi, take a nap in nice private seating areas, charge your mobile equipment, and on and on with the luxuries of exclusive airport lounges. But you either have to be a member through an airline loyalty program, credit card loyalty perks, etc. or pay $75 plus for a few hours. It might be worth it to some, but we are trying to save some money here, yet enjoy the luxuries of life too. Right?

Well, good news for you is that there are ways to enjoy airport lounges worldwide, without exclusive membership but they will come with some options to consider. Check out:

- *Plaza Network*: Plaza-Network.com –
Premium access U.S. and International lounges

- *Priority Pass*: www.prioritypass.com
The ultimate service that offers access to over 1200 lounges worldwide

- *Lounge Buddy*- https://www.loungebuddy.com/
Purchase lounge passes to access lounges worldwide for as low as $25.

- *Lounge Pass* - www.loungepass.com - VIP airport lounge access from $19

- *Day Pass* - https://daypassapp.com/ - DayPass is an on-demand day pass reservation service to luxury hotel pools, fitness centers, cabanas, beach clubs, resorts and spa facilities without the obligation of an overnight stay.

I know what a layover is, but what is a stopover?

Now on to the really cool stuff. A layover typically refers to a connection point between cities, they can be a short as 30 minutes or up to 24 hours (general 3- 6 hours), whereas a stopover refers to staying longer than 24 hours in any given city when traveling internationally. For example, you can fly from Los Angeles to Paris with a stopover in Germany. The exciting part about this is that with a stopover, especially when traveling internationally, is that you can have the opportunity to tour the city that stopover is in. You can think of it as two or more trips in one. That's how I like to look at it. I want to get the best bang for my buck.

So, if it is for only 24 hours and you land late at night, you might not want to be Dora the Explorer as you would probably want to stay near or at the airport in that case. Besides, you will probably be too tired. But if it is more than 24 hours, then get ready to ripe the tides! Go for it!

Even cooler than that is that there are websites out there that will allow you to plan your international trip and include stopovers, some for as low as $100 and you can pick the number of days that you'd like the stopover to be before you continue your trip. Yes, you can do this. Isn't that so cool? You also can choose more than one stopover location. Another option is what some airlines call Open Jaw or Round Robin flights. Open Jaw flights is when you fly into one city and fly out of another. It's like putting two one-way flights together, whereas a Round Robin is a round trip with a stopover included. It's like taking multiple trips in one. That's some serious bang for your buck.

Take a look at the following:

Air Treks: www.airtreks.com - Air Treks allows you to add multiple destinations/stops for your trip. You also get to select the days you want to spend in each location. In the example below, I selected a flight from Dallas to Paris, but I wanted to make an additional stop in Morocco then return back to Dallas. This trip would be a total of 3 continents and within a reasonable budget per person.

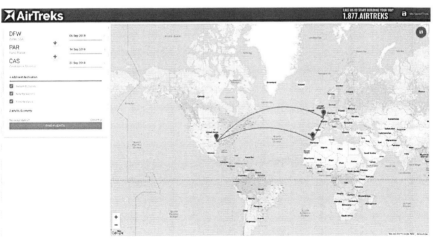

Air Wander: airwander.com - Air Wander is a great site that uses a predictive search algorithm to find the lowest prices for a flight that includes stopovers. It allows you to enter multiple stopovers just by clicking the red "plus" button. After clicking the stopover button, all the predicable stopover locations appear, and you and add the number of days that you'd like to stay in each place. Airwander also gives you the additional rates to help you estimate what the trip cost will be.

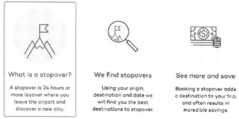

What is a stopover?	We find stopovers	See more and save
A stopover is 24 hours or more layover where you leave the airport and discover a new city.	Using your origin, destination and date we will find you the best destinations to stopover.	Booking a stopover adds a destination to your trip, and often results in incredible savings.

Departure from Atlanta to Santorini

	March 2019							April 2019					
SUN	MON	TUE	WED	THU	FRI	SAT	SUN	MON	TUE	WED	THU	FRI	SAT
					1	2		1 $382	2 $389	3 $415	4 $428	5 $429	6 $395
3	4	5	6	7	8	9	7 $417	8 $384	ATL - JTR 9 $407	10 $375	11 $423	12 $412	13 $447
10	11	12	13	14	15	16	14 $470	15 $471	16 $410	17 $440	18 $449	19 $494	20 $473
17	18	19	20	21	22	23	JTR - ATL 21	22	23	24	25	26	27
24	25	26	27	TODAY 28	29 $366	30 $352	28	29	30				
31 $378													

This flight is from Atlanta to Santorini, Greece (JTR Airport) and the available stopovers. For this particular trip, I decided to include a 3 day stopover in Reykjavik, Iceland.

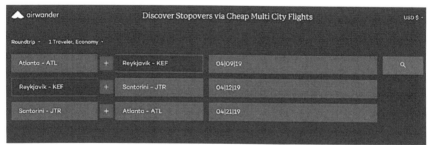

The site returns all the available options and the flight times. You can study over the available flight plans and choose the best one that will suit your schedule. *Be sure to click "Show details" to get the flight specifics.

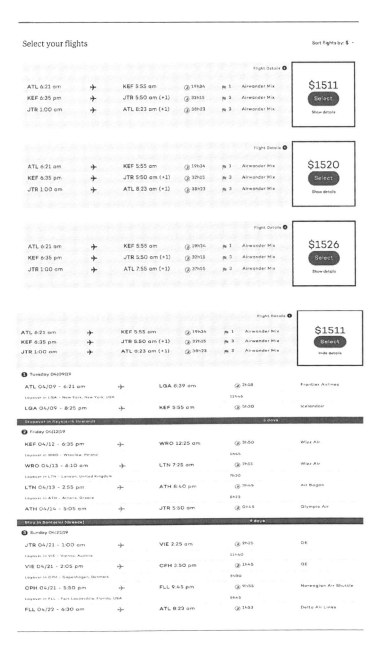

						Flight Details ●
ATL 6:21 am	✈	KEF 5:55 am	⏱ 19h34	✈ 1	Airwander Mix	**$1511**
KEF 6:35 pm	✈	JTR 5:50 am (+1)	⏱ 32h15	✈ 3	Airwander Mix	Select
JTR 1:00 am	✈	ATL 8:23 am (+1)	⏱ 38h23	✈ 3	Airwander Mix	Show details

						Flight Details ●
ATL 6:21 am	✈	KEF 5:55 am	⏱ 19h34	✈ 1	Airwander Mix	**$1520**
KEF 6:35 pm	✈	JTR 5:50 am (+1)	⏱ 32h15	✈ 3	Airwander Mix	Select
JTR 1:00 am	✈	ATL 8:23 am (+1)	⏱ 38h23	✈ 3	Airwander Mix	Show details

						Flight Details ●
ATL 6:21 am	✈	KEF 5:55 am	⏱ 19h34	✈ 1	Airwander Mix	**$1526**
KEF 6:35 pm	✈	JTR 5:50 am (+1)	⏱ 32h15	✈ 3	Airwander Mix	Select
JTR 1:00 am	✈	ATL 7:55 am (+1)	⏱ 37h55	✈ 3	Airwander Mix	Show details

						Flight Details ●
ATL 6:21 am	✈	KEF 5:55 am	⏱ 19h34	✈ 1	Airwander Mix	**$1511**
KEF 6:35 pm	✈	JTR 5:50 am (+1)	⏱ 32h15	✈ 3	Airwander Mix	Select
JTR 1:00 am	✈	ATL 8:23 am (+1)	⏱ 38h23	✈ 3	Airwander Mix	Hide details

❶ Tuesday 04/09/19

ATL 04/09 - 6:21 am	✈	LGA 8:39 am	⏱ 2h18	Frontier Airlines
Layover in LGA - New York, New York, USA			11h46	
LGA 04/09 - 8:25 pm	✈	KEF 5:55 am	⏱ 5h30	Icelandair

Stopover in Reykjavik (Iceland) — 3 days

❷ Friday 04/12/19

KEF 04/12 - 6:35 pm	✈	WRO 12:25 am	⏱ 3h50	Wizz Air
Layover in WRO - Wroclaw, Poland			5h45	
WRO 04/13 - 6:10 am	✈	LTN 7:25 am	⏱ 7h15	Wizz Air
Layover in LTN - London, United Kingdom			7h30	
LTN 04/13 - 2:55 pm	✈	ATH 8:40 pm	⏱ 3h45	Air Bagon
Layover in ATH - Athens, Greece			8h25	
ATH 04/14 - 5:05 am	✈	JTR 5:50 am	⏱ 0h45	Olympic Air

Stay in Santorini (Greece) — 9 days

❸ Sunday 04/21/19

JTR 04/21 - 1:00 am	✈	VIE 2:25 am	⏱ 2h25	OE
Layover in VIE - Vienna, Austria			11h40	
VIE 04/21 - 2:05 pm	✈	CPH 3:50 pm	⏱ 1h45	OE
Layover in CPH - Copenhagen, Denmark			2h00	
CPH 04/21 - 5:50 pm	✈	FLL 9:45 pm	⏱ 9h55	Norwegian Air Shuttle
Layover in FLL - Fort Lauderdale, Florida, USA			8h45	
FLL 04/22 - 6:30 am	✈	ATL 8:23 am	⏱ 1h53	Delta Air Lines

Clever Layover: www.cleverlayover.com - Clever Layover lets you set your own layover length at the airport you are traveling to. The site searches various airports around the world and identifies the one's based on your destination with the longest layover times.

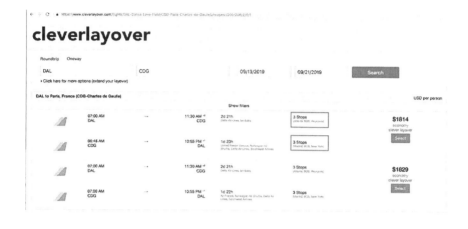

Spare of the Moment:

Check out *Airfare Watchdog's* TOP 50 FARES OF THE DAY:
https://www.airfarewatchdog.com/top-50-fares/?source=79475;

You can even set your city and see your top fares from your city.

The main thing that you need to consider when trying to grab the deals are the dates that you can fly and the airlines, which is listed under each deal. Most of the trips are roundtrip (RT).

Top Fares from your city:

In the example below, a roundtrip flight from Charlotte, NC to Tampa, FL is $74. Even though this particular route, from city to city, is only a day drive (8 hours), you can actually save on gas, possible delays, or any other issues that come along with driving from state to state.

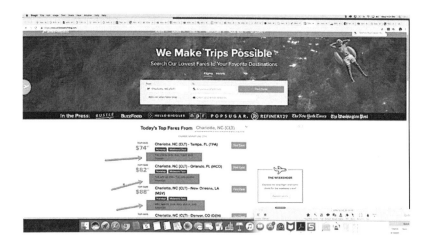

In addition to the Top Flights from your destination, Airfare Watchdog publishes *Weekend Deals:*

Room Key: *Room Key* gives you access to low Loyalty Member Rates for more than 60 of the world's largest hotel chains all in one place. Loyalty Rates are rates typically reserved for members of the hotel's loyalty program available mainly on the hotel's own website. Now Room Key is the only travel site where customers can shop and compare Loyalty Rates across so many hotel chains all in one place.

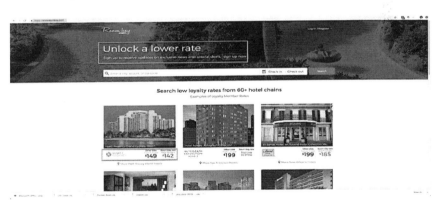

Scout by Room Key: *Scout* gives you access to exclusive hotel rates to find you a better deal. Unlock a Lower Rate. Features: Streamlined Search, Automatic Notifications, Easy Booking.

One of my favorite newly discovered app is **Skylap** (www.skylap.co). You can enter your departure airport and a general country or destination and it will return various stopovers for the length of your travel. This is super cool! I entered a flight query from Charlotte, NC to Europe for 8 days and it returned a variety of options. In this example, a person is able to travel for 8 days and visit Norway, England, and Iceland and then return home for only $1008 RT in total (no additional fees). Isn't that amazing?! Your options are limitless. Anything is possible!!

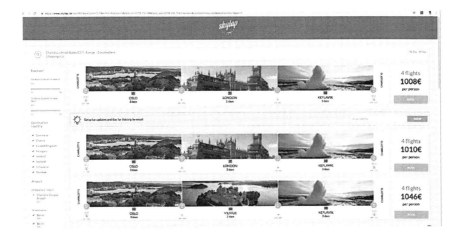

3 Alternatives to traditional hotels

1. *Traditional Bed and Breakfasts* - Not AirBnB, but traditional bed and breakfast locations that offer the extra perks of welcoming accommodations, breakfast, and more personalized service. Here are a couple of websites to refer to:

Search the site for Bed and Breakfast locations across the globe: www.bedandbreakfast.com

Black Owned Bed and Breakfast:
http://www.akwaaba.com/
or
https://travelnoire.com/black-owned-bed-and-breakfasts-across-the-u-s/

2. *Vacation Rental Homes* - This is a home away from home, separate rooms for family/friends, kitchen and dining areas, loaded cabinets and/or pantries, washer and dryer, extra amenities - all under one roof!

These are some of the most popular sites for Vacation Rental Homes:

- Vacation Rental By Owner: VRBO.com
- Home Away: HomeAway.com
- FlipKey: FlipKey.com

3. *Renting Timeshares* - You don't necessarily have to buy a timeshare to use a timeshare. There are sites out there that you can rent timeshares.

- Red Week: RedWeek.com
- Wyndham Vacation Rentals: https://www.wyndhamvacationrentals.com/
- Extra Holidays by Wyndham: https://www.extraholidays.com/
- Endless Vacation Rentals: https://www.endlessvacationrentals.com/

3 tips for using Airbnb effectively

1. *Research and read the reviews*. If I choose to stay at an Airbnb, my standard protocol is to make sure it is not a new listing but that individuals have stellar reviews, ultimately 30 plus. The more reviews the better the consistency in what to expect. Reading reviews also educates you on what you need to know about the area and sometimes things to do.

2. *Read and understand all the rules, stay respectful and treat it as if it were your own home or property.* Some people think that because it isn't their property, that they can leave it a certain way. Maybe its just me, but whether using an Airbnb or staying at a hotel I try to keep things as tidy as possible as it reflection of respecting others. I find

that when I have done this in the past, I'm always welcomed back. The hosts response to your stay tell it all.

3. *Location, Location, Location* - As it goes in real estate lingo, so the same goes for Airbnb locations. For your personal safety you want to make sure that you are not far from the airport, the main districts, or close to local transportation.

Where and How to find the best places to eat

One of the first places I refer to when trying to find the best restaurants to eat at when traveling is Yelp (www.yelp.com). I can study all the food pics and reviews, the menus and even determine what to eat as well as get a good feel of the atmosphere. Oftentimes, when you have these things in mind, dine with confidence.

Eating solo in a foreign land is really no different than doing so in your own hometown. Own It! Make small talk with the staff and maybe others around. Act like you live there. Listen, no one will ever know that you aren't from there if you don't tell them.

Other Food Apps/Websites:

GrubHub - www.grubhub.com
Open Table - www.opentable.com
Zagat - www.zagat.com
Zomoto - www.zomoto.com
Chef's Feed - www.chefsfeed.com
Four Square - www.foursquare.com
Restaurants dot com - Restaurants.com

How to not look like a tourist and blend in with the locals

Answer: Study the culture. This is especially for women solo travelers. Find a way to blend in. I will never forget the first time, in my mid-teens, that I was traveling alone to Las Vegas to visit my aunt and cousins for Christmas. I had to go through DFW (Dallas-Ft. Worth) which is a very huge airport. My granny had given me a few pointers and told me to look ahead at the signs but not to stand around like I'm lost but just walk confidently. That always stuck with me and it worked!

How to get the guts to solo travel

There is no simple formula to solo travel but just to get out there and do it. My personal tips as I've tried to share with you throughout this guide is to do as much research as possible about where you are going, map out a plan, and go ahead and take a leap of faith and just do it. Some of you have indeed travelled solo by going on trips for your work or maybe you have moved to another city different from your hometown, or went off to college. The process is no different. In fact, I have heard and have personally experienced the most eye-opening, freeing, and most peaceful places one can be in life.

Connecting with others – travel groups (Online and locally)

Some of the best ways to help motivate you along the way is to connect with others who either have some travel experiences under their belt or are a bit of a novice to the whole idea and are out there asking questions that may spark your interests as well. I've found the most inspiration through online travel groups because people love to share their experiences, in fact the pictures alone are enough to ask your own self, "What's stopping me?"

Travel groups or forums are online breeding grounds for globe trotters in the making. If you connect with the right ones, you don't have to travel to places alone but with a travel group. I've heard many reviews on how people enjoyed travel groups so much that they would continue to join the group on annual trips plus they've made lifelong friends.

The power of the # (Hashtags)

A great way to start researching social media sites for travel related posts is to use hashtags. The more direct and specific the hashtag is, the better the results. You can use hashtags in Google searches, as well as with Facebook, Twitter, or Instagram. Oftentimes when you enter one hashtag, you will get a list of related hashtags.

Here are some popular travel hashtags to start with:

#Travel, #DigitalNomads, #Vacation, #TravelHacks, #SoloTravel er, #SoloTravel, #PassportReady, #WomenWhoTravel, #TravelGoals, #Wanderlust, #TravelBlogger, #RoomWithAView, #LuxuryTravel, #LuxuryHotels, #ViewFromAbove #PostcardsFromTheWorld, #TravelCouple

Twitter Lists

Using Twitter Lists can be a great way to organize tweets in order to filter out the "noise". In the following example, I show you how I created a "Travel Deals" list.

To add to your selection, all you have to do is type what you would like to add to your list and it will return options that you can select from. Some ideas for your Twitter lists could be "budget travel", "travel blogger", "travel hacks", "travel deals" and so on... The members section lists the profiles that I selected to be a part of my list.

This is just a sample of the lists that I created.

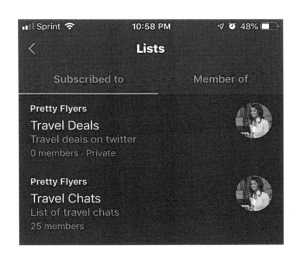

When I select a particular list, it will show the associated tweets thus eliminating the need to go through a whole Twitter feed.

Facebook Groups

Facebook Travel Groups have been my secret sauce for travel inspiration, suggestions and tips. To access Facebook travel groups, just simply enter the word "travel" in the search box and select "Groups" from the menu bar. The best way to determine good travel groups to join is to look at the number of members as well as active posts per day.

One of my best experiences using a travel group was trying to find a nice destination for a last-minute solo trip. A few people had suggested the island of Curacao - Willemstad to be exact. Honestly, I had never heard of it, but decided to do some research. All I had to do was Google it and the rest was history. I had to see if this was real. (Google for yourself and see what I mean or look at the pictures further down in this section - if you are an ebook reader).

I had asked a few people about this island and a lot of people suggested it. One particular lady had responded to my post and stated that she had just returned from there. She had offered suggestions and messaged me directly to give me more details. She even had given me the name of a dedicated taxi driver "Curacao

Taxi Max" and even reached out to him to let him know that I would be headed that way. Let's just say that the rest was history. He was my ambassador for the majority of the trip.

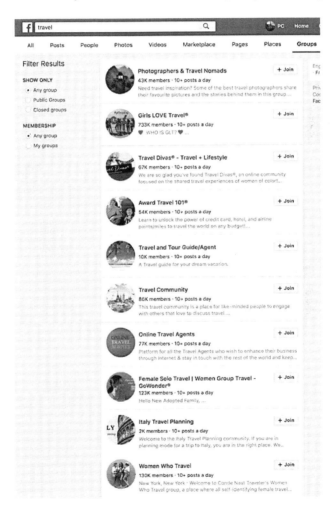

Here is part of my list of groups that I am a member of. Feel free to join me. Hope to see ya there!

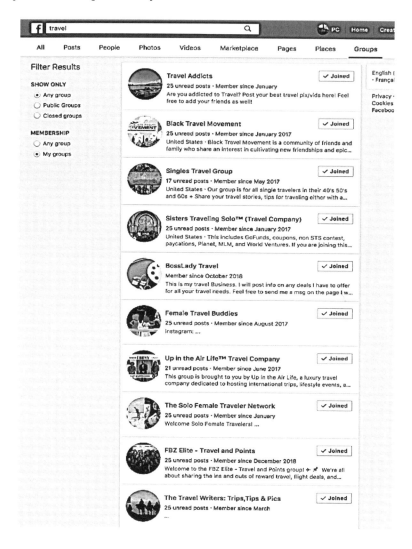

My original posts to one of the groups about going to Curacao.

Oh yeah, here is Willemstad, Curacao... see what I mean?
(Google it to see it in full color!!!)

Instagram

I use Instagram to follow various travel bloggers and travel websites who have an IG page. There are quite a few influencers on Instagram so you will never run out of inspiration.

Instagram now allows users to follow hashtags. This is another great way to filter out posts and explore a plethora of options.

Read! Read! Read!

Reviews – The good, the bad, and the ugly – (ex. Trip Advisor, Yelp, Google search)

Whether I am looking for a new restaurant to try, a hotel or other lodging, a business or destination, I read reviews because I want to make the best selection as possible and get an idea of what to expect. The key to using reviews for making a great decision is to find the options that have a lot of reviews. No less than 30 but the higher and more diverse the better.

Even if my selection has 100 good reviews and 10 fair to bad reviews, I make sure that I read them all. I try to keep in mind that all that glitters is not gold but reading allows me to use my best judgement.

Trip Advisor is a gold mine. I've used this website for almost as long as it's been around. You can join forums and ask more direct questions from followers or just read general reviews.

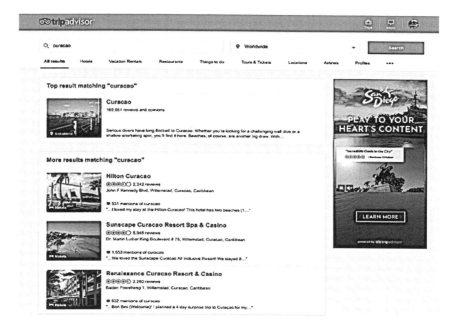

Cruise Critic - *www.cruisecritic.com* allows you to review actual cruise ships and the cruisers experiences. This site is extremely helpful for first time and seasoned cruisers alike.

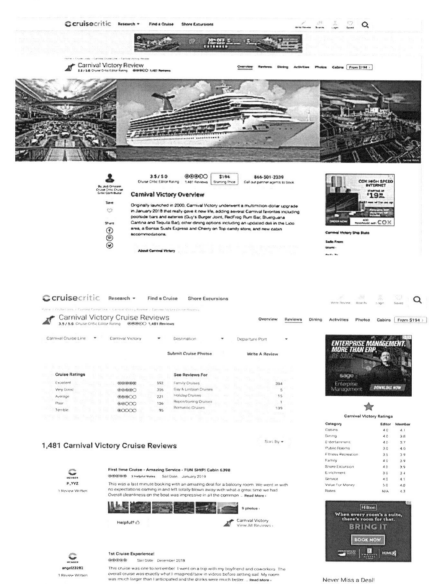

Yelp - www.yelp.com is excellent for learning about restaurant experiences.

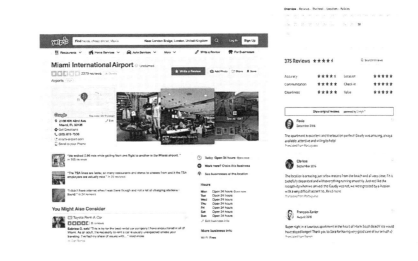

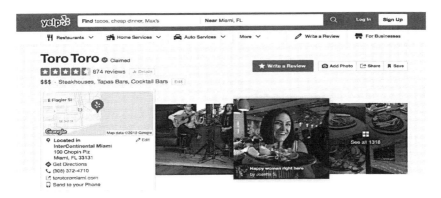

Almost any business or service that you use has an option for reviews. Make sure that you read them well. You will be better prepared, well informed, and you might even learn a tip or two that can save you both time and money.

Turo and Silvercar

SILVERCAR
by Audi

So, most of you know of the on demand personal driver services: Uber, Lyft but what if you just like the idea of having a rental car so that you have greater control of your time? There are incumbent car rental services like Enterprise, Hertz, Budget, Alamo but there are very unconventional car services like *Turo* (a peer to peer car sharing marketplace https://turo.com/), in which car owners rent out/share their personal cars to others, most are secondary cars of the owners but it is a cool concept. It's a part of the sharing ecosystem.

Skip the rental counter

I've seen everything from luxury and high-end sports cars like Bentleys, Lamborghinis, Porches, to Toyota's, Chevy's, Trucks, Jeeps, you name it. So, if you want to ride around in style and only pay a fraction of the cost, Turo is a great option. They offer a mobile app, which I recommend downloading, if you are going to use the service in order to stay in touch with the owner, etc. The system works very similar to a rental car company; it goes through an insurance check and driver record validation.

Once everything is approved in the system you and the car host will determine a location to meet you (airport, parking lot, public location). At the time of pickup, they recommend that you inspect the car and take pictures of any dents or dings prior to your rental.

Silvercar (https://www.silvercar.com/)is modern car rental service with two unique selling points: 1) They only rent out Audi's...Yes, Audi's. 2) Make your reservations through their mobile app (recommended) or on their website. You will need to set up a profile but once you're done, you are set and ready to go. When you arrive at the *Silvercar* kiosk located at the car rental center, all you have to do is pull up your info. Your car will already be reserved so all you have to do is get it and go! Zoom Zoom!

They currently service major cities throughout the US, so make sure that you check them out.

Car Sharing Economy

Another option that I've used is Turo. Turo is a part of the sharing economy but in the car space. It's definitely an alternative to rental cars. Turo is the Airbnb of rental cars. I had used this option once in Los Angeles by booking though their mobile app. (There is also a website option, but the mobile app is more convenient).

I was a little nervous about the process and what the experience would be like, but it was as smooth as booking through a rental website. The site/app validates your driving record and insurance but other than that, the renter approves your request to book and that's it.
Pick up was easy. The renter met me at the airport with the car and I took pictures of it like I would have with a regular rental so that I could have proof and timestamp of any marks or dents so that I would not be liable for anything. In fact, the renter had pointed out the marks and suggested I'd do so.

When it was about time return the car, I simply messaged the renter and he told me where to meet him to drop the car back off, which in this particular situation, we met in a parking lot adjacent to the airport, simply because the LAX is too busy. Besides, I had my uncle and aunt right there making sure I got back to the airport safely.

Note to self: Never rent a Mini Coupe for driving in a city like LA. You need something a little more 'Fast and Furious' like a Karma Revero 2019. Have you heard of that? Well, me neither but it's a snazzy little something. Go look it up! In fact, renting from Turo while visiting places like LA or Miami is the best time to splurge. Like, Live Your Life!! You saved on airfare and lodging, why not drive around in class every now and then. Even if it's for a day.

Husbands, Wives, Significant Others, go ahead and spoil your love on your getaways. How extra romantic would that be? Ladies, if your anything like me, if I were treated to something so special, chile...I'd leave all my packed clothes and go get some extra classy numbers and grace the city like Audrey Hepburn or the Duchess of Cambridge or Sussex with the Naomi Campbell signature walk.

Okay, back to Turo...You can find some super fancy cars on this site from the Karma Revero to the BMW i8, Rolls Royce Ghost or Dawn, Maserati Quattroporte, or Bentley Continental GTC. Maybe it's just me, but I don't come from a place with all these fancy cars passing me on the highways and byways so hey, might as well go for the gold.

You might think that this option is a little unsafe or you might be a little unsure but if you've ever gotten an Uber then what's the difference? You got me? As always, I believe in and will always promote safety first and caution anyone to always let someone know your whereabouts just in case anything happens.

* I might have mentioned this earlier but if you have any type of phone tracking device that you can enable during your travels that a family member or friend can keep up with your whereabouts, then use it. I had a friend once suggest that to me and it just made sense. On the iPhone, it's either Find My Friends or Location Sharing option. Simply Brilliant!

Finally, if you are an Audi lover, there's a rental car service that you can rent nothing but Audi's. It's called Silver Car www.silvercar.com. It's another alternative to the traditional rental car service. All you have to do is download the app, sign up and select an option and unlock the car. You can rent an Audi A4 or Audi Q5 starting at $99 per day, but if it is your first time using the service, you can get 20% off. Sure, it's on the steeper end of the price for rentals but if you are splurging a bit then this is an option.

Best of all, these options are included in the cost of your rental:

- Navigation
- Wi-Fi + Bluetooth
- Fair Fuel Plan + Toll Tracking
- Apple CarPlay + Android Auto
- Child seats
- Ski racks
- Insurance Cover - option to use your own whether Personal or Corporate, or you can use their selected service

Currently, Silver Car is available in 25 locations and many popular US cities.

Other sites to check out for discount rental cars are:

www.hotwire.com
www.priceline.com
www.orbitz.com
www.ladybug.com

It's best to shop around and compare deals and when you're ready to purchase, snag it.

Discount on Rental Cars

Whenever I need to rent a car, I always check to see if I can find a good deal. One of the first places that I start is RentalCarMomma.com and because I am a Budget Rental Car Fastbreak Member, I always check to see if there are any offer codes available that will allow me to get a great discount and/or a decent upgrade for the same price.

I like Budget for several reasons, one is their Fastbreak membership which allows you to show your driver's license, pick up your keys and GO! Also, when you return your rental, all you have to do is park the car in the designated area and proceed to the airport. They will email you the receipt and you can check everything as you make a mad dash to the airport. I know this option has been great for me in times when I am cutting it close. Yes, I confess I have even had them call my name at the gate, maybe once in my whole travel life time, but if you happen to run into any snags or delays, the last thing that you have to think about is standing in a long line trying to return your rental.

Budget also has an option in which you can Pay Now or Pay Later. If you select Pay Now, there is an instant discount worthy of grabbing right then and there. There have been times that I have selected the Pay Later option so that I can hold that offer and shop around a bit more just in case I stumble upon a better offer.

Please note that you may even get the best deal by going directly through the rental car website, even on sporty cars. Plus, I use my AAA membership for additional discount. Thanks to my momma using AAA since I could remember, I carry on the legacy. Hey, don't judge me, it has come into great use if I must say so myself.

International Travel Tips

Here are some important tips to keep in mind before traveling outside of the United States.

This information is directly from the **U.S. Department of State - Bureau of Consular Affairs** website located at https://travel.state.gov/content/travel/en/international-travel/before-you-go/travelers-checklist.html

Emergency Assistance

Sometimes, in spite of careful planning, things still go wrong during a trip abroad. We provide help for emergencies **24 hours a day, 7 days a week**.

Contact the nearest U.S. embassy or consulate overseas or our Washington, D. C. office
(**888-407-4747 or 202-501-4444**).

International Travel Contacts
Getting Help in an Emergency
What can you do to get help in an emergency?
Contact the nearest U.S. embassy or consulate, or call these numbers in the United States:

- From the U.S. & Canada - 1-888-407-4747
- From Overseas - +1 202-501-4444

Report a Lost or Stolen Passport:

- From the U.S. & Canada 1-888-407-4747
- From Overseas +1 202-501-4444

Travel Safety

Review the Travel Advisories page for a listing of safety warnings in the countries that you would be traveling to. Please make sure to take the necessary precautions as advised.

There are four Travel Advisory Levels:

1. Exercise normal precautions
2. Exercise increased precautions
3. Reconsider Travel
4. Do not Travel

Below is a snapshot of the actual Travel Advisories page from travel.state.gov. You can either search by entering a country name or scrolling through the pages. As you notice in this example, the first option has a Level 4 notice, which is the highest level labeling it as "Do Not Travel" location. Should you choose to learn of more information regarding the travel advisory, just click on the particular country name.

You might notice on the third screenshot, a message from the embassy notification. This is especially important, because wherever you travel internationally, an US embassy is going to be your first point of contact in the case of an emergency. I know that this might be a little detailed, but it might come in handy for someone especially if you are traveling solo or even with young children.

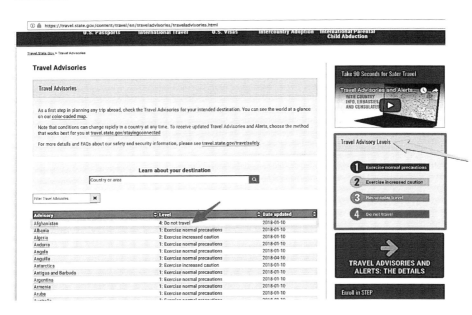

Even if you are traveling to a location that has low to normal travel precautions, it is good to check out some of the various reports and information. In the following example, I selected Curacao and noticed that it has a Level 1 travel advisory, which is to "Exercise normal precautions", however, I wanted to know what that might entail for this selection.

The information available gives me options for Country Information page which includes good things to know but it also gives me a Crime and Safety report. This is especially good so that you can identify what the common trend is and how to take precaution.

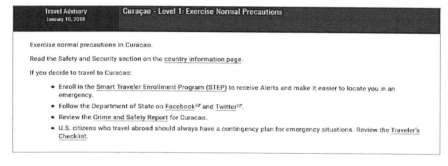

Advisory	Level	Date updated
Cuba	3: Reconsider travel	2018-03-02
Curacao	1: Exercise normal precautions	2018-01-10
Cyprus	1: Exercise normal precautions	2018-01-10
Czech Republic	1: Exercise normal precautions	2018-01-10

Curacao Travel Advisory

Travel Advisory January 10, 2018	Curaçao - Level 1: Exercise Normal Precautions

Exercise normal precautions in Curacao.

Read the Safety and Security section on the country information page.

If you decide to travel to Curacao:

- Enroll in the Smart Traveler Enrollment Program (STEP) to receive Alerts and make it easier to locate you in an emergency.
- Follow the Department of State on Facebook and Twitter.
- Review the Crime and Safety Report for Curacao.
- U.S. citizens who travel abroad should always have a contingency plan for emergency situations. Review the Traveler's Checklist.

Travel.State.Gov > International Travel > Country Information > Curaçao

Curaçao
Curaçao
Last Updated: November 8, 2017

Travel Advisory January 10, 2018	Curaçao - Level 1: Exercise Normal Precautions

Exercise normal precautions in Curacao.

... [READ MORE]

Embassy Messages	Alerts

View Alerts and Messages Archive

Quick Facts

PASSPORT VALIDITY:	VACCINATIONS:
Must be valid for duration of trip. More information on entry requirements may be found here.	None
BLANK PASSPORT PAGES:	**CURRENCY RESTRICTIONS FOR ENTRY:**
One page required for entry stamp	None
TOURIST VISA REQUIRED:	**CURRENCY RESTRICTIONS FOR EXIT:**
None	None

Educating yourself as much as possible about the location that you will be traveling to is key whether domestic or international.

Global Entry is a U.S. Customs and Border Protection (CBP) program that allows expedited clearance for pre-approved, low-risk travelers upon arrival in the United States. Members enter the United States through automatic kiosks at select airports.

Costs: A $100 non-refundable fee. Membership is good for five years.

Benefits:

- Allows you to skip the lines at passport control and customs when entering the United States

- TSA Precheck which is for scanning yourself and your carry-on baggage, but having this option available allows you to move through a separate line, much faster, plus you don't have to remove your shoes or empty your bag. This especially comes in handy, especially if you are running late in a large crowded airport (not that you should practice running late, but it does help!)

To apply, go to the US Customs and Borders Protection website: https://www.cbp.gov/travel/trusted-traveler-programs/global-entry/how-apply

Communicating back home

Need the ability to contact back home but don't want to incur all the service charges and roaming feels from your mobile service carrier? Use WhatsApp. WhatsApp is a messaging service app that allows you to text, make calls for free (check with your carrier if any data charges are applicable) as well as send voice text messages back and forth. I found this quite handy when I was visiting Curacao. It was how I communicated with my Ambassador/Taxi Driver, my Airbnb host, along with friends that I had met on the island. In fact, I use it to keep in touch since I've been back home.

I would definitely recommend downloading this app before you leave and make sure that your friends and families have WhatsApp installed on their mobile devices.

You can learn more about WhatsApp by going to their website: https://www.whatsapp.com/

Know your embassy

This is an important point and I thought that it was worth sharing, specifically for those traveling outside of the country. With the ... that we've seen and many travelers have experienced being caught in the midst of a state of emergency and needing assistance to get home.

Locate the Embassy

This is an important point and I thought that it was worth sharing, specifically for those traveling outside of the country. With the recent weather phenomenon over that past couple of years, through hurricanes, earthquakes, and the like that we've seen and many travelers have experienced being caught in the midst of a state of emergency and needing assistance to get home, it's important to know what to do and who to contact. That is where the US Embassy comes into play.

What is a U.S. Embassy and how can it be of resource for me while traveling?

When you are going on vacation to a foreign country for the first time, you will want to do some research in advance. While doing this research, and talking to friends who have been on vacation in a foreign country before, you may hear the term "embassy" pop up here and there. Most people have a slight idea what a U.S. embassy is. But what do they really do? And are they going to play any role in your vacation to another country?

So where can you find a US Embassy while in a foreign country? One thing to note is that they are almost always located in the capital city of the foreign country. This is likely because the ambassador must frequently meet with politicians and important officials. The embassy is typically a compound with many buildings, and a large American flag outside. The exact location of an embassy can be found online. It's important to write down the address and phone number of the U.S. embassy in the country you plan to visit. It's always good to be prepared for whatever might happen.

U.S. Consulate General in Amsterdam by iampixels/DepositPhotos

While the Consular officers provide immediate and personal assistance to American citizens every day around the world:

- replacing lost passports

95

- assisting injured or ill travelers
- and assisting with marriages, births, and adoptions
- other sections of the embassy provide more specialized assistance

Website: https://www.usembassy.gov/

Since this is an extensive list, you can view this info on the My Travel Black Book App or Digital Version to access the links directly:

No Passport Needed Islands

Haven't gotten around to getting your passport yet but you really want to travel to a beautiful island which you've always dreamed of going to? Before I give you some of the places to go, skip down to the next section about getting your passport. No more delays okay?

Now that you've applied for your passport and waiting to receive it, you've got an itch to visit an island, sooner than later. Okay, I've got you covered.

Well, here are some of the islands that you can visit:

The beautiful and I mean beautiful postcard picture perfect *U.S. Virgin Islands: St. John, St. Croix and St. Thomas.* You can also visit *Puerto Rico, Guam,* and the *American Samoa Islands.* Another option is to take a cruise if you are departing from and returning to a U.S. port. The only thing that you must consider if doing so is if you have an emergency and need to fly back from the island, then you will need a passport, so keep that in mind. A passport is worth the investment even if you don't use often, it's a great secondary form of identity.

I really want to encourage you to
GO GET YOUR PASSPORT TODAY!

Take a moment right now and go to the U.S. Department of State – Bureau of Consular Affairs website and apply. (https://travel.state.gov/content/travel/en/passports.html) I recommend that you grab your birth certificate (or record of citizenship), driver's license or other valid forms of legal identification such as your social security card and have it handy. It's as simple as filling out a job application, well maybe not that extensive, you don't have to list your previous employers or references, but what I am getting at is that applying for your passport is pretty simple. NO MORE EXCUSES OKAY?

I know in times past that filling your passport book with stamps of all the places you've visited was the thing to do; however, many countries no longer make that a requirement, which is a little disappointing. Nonetheless, you can take plenty of pictures and grab some souvenirs for memories.

Passport Costs:

For First-time passport applicants, the fees are as follows:

First-time Adult Passport Book –
$110 (Application Fee) $35 (Execution Fee)

First-time Adult Passport Card –
$30 (Application Fee); $35 (Execution Fee)

First-time Adult Passport Book and Passport Card –
$140 (Application Fee); $35 (Execution Fee)

*** You will need to reference the actual government website for accurate fees. **

Travel Quote

Your passport is your key to explore
the world! Go. See. Do."
- Brilliant Wanderer

Pay attention to the details

(This is more comical than anything, but still has an underlying message! ☺)

Pay attention to where you are going, especially in large cities with multiple airports. True Story: A few years ago, I had traveled to Houston, Texas and being that I lived there for a portion of my life, I was familiar with the main airports there which would be George Bush Intercontinental Airport in North Houston and Houston Hobby in South Houston. My friend, Monica, was picking me up from the airport so I figured this would be easy breezy…Not! I must have been super excited to be going somewhere because out of booking the flight and through the whole air travel experience, I had considered nothing else except that I was going to Houston. I didn't see it on the computer screen when I booked my flight, neither on the ticket, nor on the monitors at the gates, not even on the plane as we were making our final descent. Nothing.

She had even asked me several times which airport I was flying into and I confidentially stated Houston Hobby. I arrived in

"Houston" safely but had actually thought that the airport where I landed had been renovated since it had been quite a while since I had flown into the city. I figured that this was a new annex and it would take me a minute or so to get my bearings. However, my friend and I were on the phone and she had described her car and location and for me to exit the building. I stood out there for about 15 minutes while she kept driving around looking for me.

Out of much exasperation, she asked me if I was really at the correct airport. I calmly reassured her that I was at Houston Hobby and put her on hold so that I could ask a nearby traveler. "Sir, which airport am I at?" He looked at me in bewilderment (as to say, girl you don't know what airport you are at?) and answered "Intercontinental." Oh, the shame I had felt to answer my friend and let her know that I was indeed at the wrong airport and that she would have to take about a 45-minute trip up north.

I say all that to say, pay attention to the details, even if you are great at planning and remembering information.

Travel Quote

You don't have to be rich to see the world
- Anonymous

Families

A Family That Travels Together

I wanted to dedicate this portion of the book to families as a whole. To me, there is nothing like family and to be honest that's one of the most irreplaceable parts in your life. My prayer is that at least one family would take a step toward building a stronger bond through travel and spending time together, even if it is a weekend trip to the lake. Leave all the issues including work, the phone calls, and all other distractions behind and focus on what it truly means to be family.

Laugh, dance, play, sing out loud but whatever you do, enjoy one another. Everyone plays an important role in the family unit. Father, Mother, Son and Daughter. Single Parent Families. However, your family unit is made up of, family is essential. Life is certainly precious and one of the most precious gifts you have is the gift of family.

A very good friend of mine, Arleathia "Lisa" Chambliss and her family have always inspired me with their travel journeys. I wanted to know what inspired them to travel as a family unit. The story behind it is beautiful. She and her two sisters, Cynthia Hightower and Wanda Daniels are now all travel agents with their own individual travel agencies. They are not just ordinary travel agents, but they host cruise parties and really put their all into it as they care for those they serve.

Much about that later, but I had asked Lisa to share with me her story about her family's travel journeys and their experiences. "Traveling has taught me so much. I have seen and learned about different cultures, people, communities, foods and atmospheres. We began our journey of traveling around the world because we wanted to celebrate our sister surviving breast cancer. It started out with us participating in local breast cancer races in Atlanta for an organization who raises funding for breast cancer research. After a few years of participating in that local event, my sister decided that she wanted to celebrate her 5-year milestone of being cancer free, so we planned a family trip to Washington, DC for the annual breast cancer race. The whole family went from our grandmother, mother, aunties, nephews, sisters, brother, and brother in laws. It was such an inspiration for my sister to have her family support her.

A few words from the bible in Isaiah 54:17- 'NO WEAPONS' motivated her and continued to motivate us as well. We had decided to make it our mission to participate in various races supporting different organizations which would allow us to travel around the nation. Since each of my sisters and I share the same joy of travel, we decided to start our own travel agencies. This would allow us the opportunity to spread the love and joy of traveling together that we've experienced over the years with other families. Our theme as travel agents is TAKE THE NATION ON VACATION and we are passionate about what we do and how we serve others.

Celebrating life has been our motivation, so we made a decision to travel as a family once a year. Traveling has brought us closer together more than ever. Most of my family doesn't travel as much; however, me and my sisters are agents so we get to travel more often. We have been all around the world from Paris, Dubai, Japan and Hawaii to the Caribbean Islands.
It has been a DREAM COME TRUE. I have seen a couple of Wonders of the World, including one of the natural wonders in the US, which is the Grand Canyon.

We drive (and fly) from state to state and city to city. We cruise from Caribbean Island to Caribbean Island, all the while planning cruise parties for our clients in order to keep them informed and motivated. We show our clients that we value their business by rewarding them and being there for them from the beginning until the end of the cruise. This keeps them coming back for more.

Life is short. We love being around each other and began to realize how important it is to be with family and to enjoy life together. *Our motto is: "A family who prays together is a family who loves, travels, and celebrates life together."* God said that we MUST love one another and my family believes in this command and have been obedient to His word. We love each other and there's nothing you can do about it!

After realizing how much I was missing waiting on other people to travel with, I'm no longer afraid to travel alone or with family. I enjoy living for myself more than anything. Life is good." ~ Arleathia Chambliss

I hope that Lisa's story encourages you and your loved ones to begin your journey. There are families that have travel dreams but think that they cannot afford to take a family vacation. Keep reading as you will learn how one family overcame that barrier.

— Now back to where I left off about Lisa and her sisters not being ordinary travel agents. My cousins recently married and had decided to take a cruise with family and friends for their honeymoon. I had been on a cruise previously with Lisa's family, which her sister Wanda had planned and let me tell you, they know how to do it! I had decided to reach out to Lisa for help with planning the honeymoon cruise. My cousins and their guests were in good hands from start to finish. Lisa and her other sister Cynthia had flown all the way from Atlanta to Oklahoma City to host a cruise party for the guests. First timers and experienced travelers alike were well informed and reassured of the processes, received valuable travel tips as well as assistance with any last-minute registration needs.

Lisa and Cynthia had prepared personalized goodie bags for the travelers. It was such a blast and the guests enjoyed every bit of it. How often do you have travel agents go all out of their way to serve you…Literally? If you ever need any travel agents to help you plan cruises or make family reunion, class reunion, company travel arrangements, please be sure to check these sisters out. You won't be disappointed. Their information is in the Travel Resource portion of this book.

Family of 10 to Disney for about $3500

7 adults and 3 children

A coworker friend of mine, Amie Honeycutt, shared with me her dream of taking her family, 10 people in total to Disneyland for 7 days for approximately $3500. Yes, you read that correctly. This had been on her vision board and she was able to see this dream come true. Like, who wouldn't want to spend time with family at the happiest place on earth for 7 days and in under $5000?

She shared her strategy with me and in her own words, I'd like to share them with you:

- Choose days that are the least popular for tourist times.
- We went to Disney World on a Monday and Universal on a Wednesday BEFORE Memorial Day Weekend and opted out of Park Hopper passes.
- We decided one day at each park was good enough and we wouldn't want to bounce around from park to park.
- I did NOT opt out of park hopping passes for Universal.
- We wanted to do the entire Olli Vander's Wizarding Wand Experience.
- Flying is really expensive for 10 people so we drove instead. Once you factor in bags, airfare, and then a rental (or two) to get around wasn't the cheapest route.
- Do NOT stay on the Disney World/Universal

campus with a large group of people.

- Unless you are camping (that's around $50 a night but we weren't feeling sleeping on the ground), then expect to pay an astronomical amount.
- I scored a townhome two blocks away for a grand total of $900 for 6 nights. That's a whopping total of $10 a person per night. Not too shabby.
- I also stayed on top of tickets.
- I started planning this trip well over a year before actually going so I was constantly looking for the cheapest deal.
- I highly recommend securing your tickets through a third-party booking agency but always keep your eyes on the actual Disney World and Universal websites.
- I was able to cancel my tickets through the agency and buy the Disney Tickets when they went on sale. My Universal tickets remained cheapest through the site.
- You don't have to go to Disney World and Universal for every day that you're down there.
- There is a TON of stuff to do in Florida. Keep that in mind while planning. Don't overload yourself or your family. This is a vacation after all.

Amie's tips: *"The sooner you can start planning, the better. Reserve now but don't commit until the last second. I know about $2000 off of my total by waiting."*

There you have it ladies and gentlemen. It is possible to live your dreams and give your family an experience and memories that will last a lifetime.

Other Disney Savings Resources:

Mousesavers: https://www.mousesavers.com/ - Offers discounts, deals, and coupons for Disney
Westgate Resorts:
https://www.westgatereservations.com/walt-disney-world/discount-disney-tickets/

Another option to stay in Orlando and get free or discounted tickets to Disney is to take up an offer from a timeshare. You don't have to buy but you sure get a nice place to stay, some throw in rental cars as well as Disney tickets. You will need to check with them first before you take the offer up.

Typically, all you have to do is sit in on a 90-minute presentation and the rest is yours. Keep in mind, don't be pressured into buying anything unless you choose to and that it is an option for you and your family in the future.

How to Make Your Family Vacation Affordable:

Flight Deals for Families: There are site aggregators such as www.smartfares.com that offer Family Travel Deals. Here's a scenario for a family of 5 from Dallas to LA during spring break. The lowest price found roundtrip per person is $274. That's a total of 5 airline tickets under $1500. However, you could consider options such as student fares/rates that might also reduce the cost a bit more.

Hold that thought. I've got another option for you. Check this out. Same family of 5, same destination, but the date range may vary. Be ready to pack your bags and head to Sunny LA for $100 RT per person! Yes, your whole family can fly for $500 and save approximately $1000. Isn't that awesome?

This is through the *Secret Flying*. They publish a lot of error fares and low-cost fares but the deals do not last long. You can go through their website (www.secretflying.com) but the best way to grab the deals are through their social media accounts, especially Twitter and Instagram (Facebook too). The deals are real and they are a steal but you have to read the details because they actually spell out for you how to get the deal itself. (see example below)

Non-stop flights from Dallas, Texas to Los Angeles for only $100 roundtrip with United Airlines.

Also works in reverse.

DEPART:
Dallas, USA

ARRIVE:
Los Angeles, USA

RETURN:
Dallas, USA

Saturday, February 9

Dallas > Los Angeles   3h 35m

| | United Airlines
Flight 312
Boeing 737-900 | 5:55p
Dallas, TX
DFW Dallas/Fort Worth Intl Air... | 7:30p
Los Angeles, CA
LAX Los Angeles Intl Airport | 3h 35m
Basic Economy |

Tuesday, February 12

Los Angeles > Dallas   3h 9m

| | United Airlines
Flight 5609
Embraer E175 | 6:50p
Los Angeles, CA
LAX Los Angeles Intl Airport | 11:59p
Dallas, TX
DFW Dallas/Fort Worth Intl Air... | 3h 9m
Basic Economy |

Operated by United Express/SkyWest

View what's included >

Basic Economy
MOST RESTRICTIVE

$ Seat Choice

✕ Carry-on Bag

$ Checked Bags

Selected +$0/person

◄   ►

See baggage fee information >

Continue to Checkout for $100.40/person

107

Once you select a date, click the Go to Deal button and Secret Flying will then redirect you to the website and query that will actually return that particular deal. At that moment, it's up for grabs. In this case, the site redirected to priceline.com.

It's sort of like a done for you type of service. It does the search query for you and all you have to do and pick an option and pay. Simple as that.

Wanna take your family to the Islands?

Suppose the adults in the group are yearning wander off to a beach destination different than the traditional U.S. hotspots, but you don't want to leave the kiddos behind, then check out SecretFlying.com other deals. This same family of 5 can fly to Cancun (RT) for $163 per person. (Approximately $815 total)

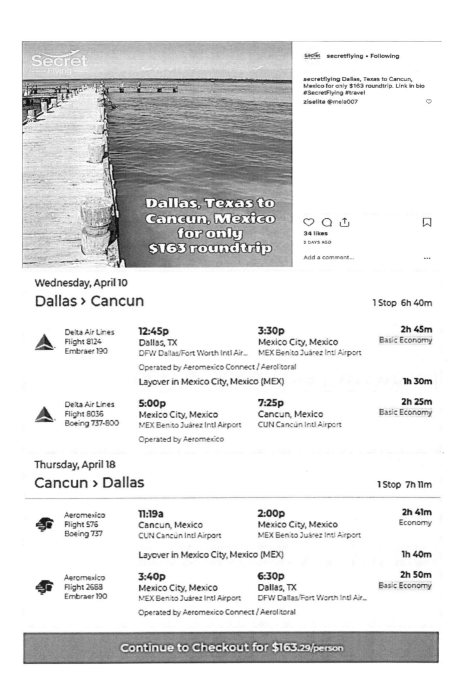

Dallas, Texas to Cancun, Mexico for only $163 roundtrip

Wednesday, April 10

Dallas > Cancun

1 Stop 6h 40m

Delta Air Lines Flight 8124 Embraer 190	**12:45p** Dallas, TX DFW Dallas/Fort Worth Intl Air...	**3:30p** Mexico City, Mexico MEX Benito Juárez Intl Airport	**2h 45m** Basic Economy

Operated by Aeromexico Connect / Aerolitoral

Layover in Mexico City, Mexico (MEX) — 1h 30m

Delta Air Lines Flight 8036 Boeing 737-800	**5:00p** Mexico City, Mexico MEX Benito Juárez Intl Airport	**7:25p** Cancun, Mexico CUN Cancún Intl Airport	**2h 25m** Basic Economy

Operated by Aeromexico

Thursday, April 18

Cancun > Dallas

1 Stop 7h 11m

Aeromexico Flight 576 Boeing 737	**11:19a** Cancun, Mexico CUN Cancún Intl Airport	**2:00p** Mexico City, Mexico MEX Benito Juárez Intl Airport	**2h 41m** Economy

Layover in Mexico City, Mexico (MEX) — 1h 40m

Aeromexico Flight 2688 Embraer 190	**3:40p** Mexico City, Mexico MEX Benito Juárez Intl Airport	**6:30p** Dallas, TX DFW Dallas/Fort Worth Intl Air...	**2h 50m** Basic Economy

Operated by Aeromexico Connect / Aerolitoral

Continue to Checkout for $163.29/person

** Please note: While the prices are low, the departure and return date range is pretty lengthy so you might consider using their

109

scenario dates, carrier and break up your trip with one-way fares. It might take a little work, but if it can save you hundreds then it is worth the effort. In the previous examples the time range was about 12 days, so unless you want to leave for a two-week vacation you might want to look at the deals closely. **

Another option to find flights, not as simple as Secret Flying but Google Flights will help you plan travel around the specific dates that you want to use and actually show you fares for different dates. The caveat of this is that if you have the flexibility to adjust your date range, then you may end up saving significantly. I entered in my original preferred travel dates and it returned what seemed to be a bit pricey $253 RT from Dallas to LA for 6 days. However, I used the price graph option to see the optional dates that would be lower and I found one for $111 RT per person. ($142 savings per person)

Trip Total: Family of 5 flying from Dallas to LA for 6 days: $555 (before taxes and fees)

See my example below:

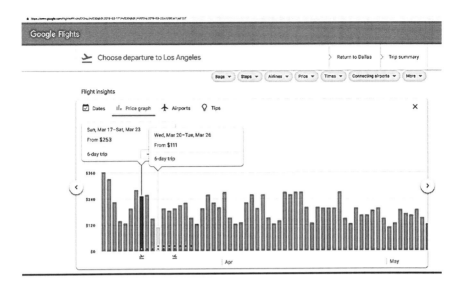

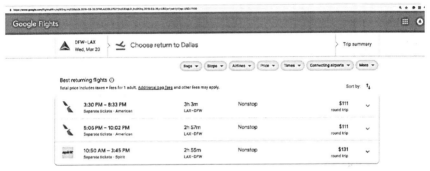

Airline Tips for Families

- Make your airline reservations early
- Stagger airline ticket reservations, especially for group travel
- Check into student discounts
- Book through a travel agency with an option to add a payment plan
- Think outside of the box and check non-airline specific websites

Consider renting an RV

The first thing that I think about with loading up a pile of people (for a road trip) in a vehicle - regardless of size is National Lampoon's Vacation or Johnson Family Vacation. These families didn't travel in style and the luxury of an RV as they were all crammed up with nowhere to go. Well, what better way to travel and see the world with family, eliminating the costs of airfare, rental cars, hotels than to rent an RV and take your home on the road.

The main costs to factor in when renting an RV are:

Cost of rental
Parking/Camping Site fee (based on the number of days) Gas

Small Tip - Before the day of departure, consider cleaning and sanitizing the whole vehicle and sleeping areas to your satisfaction, even though the owners must present the vehicles clean, doing that will give yourself a little ease and make it feel (and smell) like home.

Another awesome part about using an RV is that you can bring little extras from home that you couldn't pack with you on an airplane posing extra baggage fees or not enough trunk space in a rental car. Plus, you can also save money by buying groceries and cooking and snacking the whole trip, thus reducing the dining expenditures.

Don't want to drive? Consider hiring a professional driver. Of course you would have to check his/her credentials and background but some people do this for a living and/or for retirement income. They usually charge a flat rate depending on distance, plus the cost of a hotel room and maybe meals. Those incidentals may all be included in the fee itself.

Here are a few sites that offer RV Rentals that are the AirBnB of the RV sharing ecosystem:

RV Share - https://rvshare.com/
Outdoorsy - https://outdoorsy.com

I remember years ago, Oprah had a contest where you could write in to her about a dream that she would pick one person to fulfill. I wrote this long letter about how I really wanted my family: my mother, aunts, uncles, and cousins to get together for a unique family reunion and that we could be do so traveling to a destination in RVs. This was like the trip of all trips. I mean if you are gonna dream, you might as well dream...Right? I didn't win and never got around to doing that while my mom was living, but hopefully someone out there would be inspired to do that for their family. If so, write me and let me know. In fact, reach out to me, if you are planning to do so and I will help you brainstorm some great ideas for a RV road trip. I can dream and live vicariously through your family. Deal?

Alternative Hotel Options

A few years ago, my family and I went on a trip for Christmas to Las Vegas. It was a group of 9 and we wanted to stay in the main area while keeping it affordable. We chose the Wyndham Grand Desert Resort (https://www.wyndhamgranddesert.com/) which was less than 2 miles from The Strip. We had adjoining units (2 bedroom lock off), each unit had a kitchenette, dining area, queen size sleeper sofa in the living area as well as a master bedroom with a Queen/King size bed. The main unit even had a whirlpool bathtub.

This was absolutely a wonderful option as it kept the family together, but everyone had a place to lay their head down as well as space to move around comfortably. We were able to cook and have Christmas dinner right there in our units, my aunt actually prepared a seafood broil. Non-traditional (which is good in my book) but was so delicious!

As I mentioned earlier, the location was perfect for being able to walk to the strip or adjoining activities around. The Wyndham offered shuttle services, which was convenient and there were actually a lot more amenities that we did not even get to take advantage of. I did not go through Wyndham's website, but actually was able to find a great deal through VRBO (Vacation Rentals By Owner). Nine people were able to rent out a 2 unit for less than $500 for about 4 days. That's about $55 per person or $13 per day each. My personal preferences and needs met: Safe. Clean. Great Amenities. Spacious. Conveniently Located with a "home" feel.

Below is an idea of our layout for 9 people. We weren't all crammed together. As long as you know how to make it work, then it is possible.

This is a home that I had come across this 5-bed villa with a private pool on VRBO that is about 10 minutes away from Disney and can accommodate up to 10 people. So as mentioned earlier, you can save a bit on the expense of going out to eat every day and make meals in your home away from home. Keep it simple though, after all you are on vacation.

Here are some additional alternative hotel options comparable to VRBO:

Tripping.com - World's number one site for vacation rentals - search aggregator.

Flipkey.com - A vacation rental marketplace; offers Trip Ideas such as Girlfriends, Cheap European Destinations, Best Islands to visit.

Airbnb.com - Unforgettable trips start with Airbnb. Find adventures nearby or in faraway places and access unique homes, experiences, and places around the world.

Homeaway.com - Rent everything from cabins & condos to castles or villas.

Resortshare.com - Free full-service management and rental services for point- based timeshare owners and a better vacation for guests at exclusive resorts with great rooms.

Stay on a University Campus as a Hotel Alternative:

Yes! I did that a few years ago while visiting St. Louis for the first time. Such a great choice. I can't even tell you how I stumbled across the idea, but I did a great deal of research at the time and thought to myself, why not? I stayed at Washington University's Charles F. Knight Executive Education & Conference Center which is located on the beautiful campus of Washington University. I was there during a Memorial Day holiday weekend so the campus was pretty quiet. I actually thought that the room would be a dorm room with two twin beds, which that would have been okay, but I was so wrong. It was set up as a very nice hotel.

Don't just take my word, check out the reviews on tripadvisor.com: https://www.tripadvisor.com/Hotel_Review-g44881-d1175143-Reviews-Charles_F_Knight_Executive_Education_Conference_Center-Saint_Louis_Missouri.html (I keep referring you to tripadvisor.com because it's important to do extensive research so that you can be comfortable about your decision)

The stay included a complete breakfast which was above the traditional continental breakfast with maybe some pastries and coffee or orange juice. No, I had a selection to choose from and could have ordered more but there were limited services during the holiday weekend. Their accommodations included 66 guest rooms, lounges, and dining room.

Here are some additional resources for staying on a college campus while vacationing:

University Rooms: https://www.universityrooms.com/ - This website locates vacant rooms in university colleges and residences are cleared and cleaned in readiness for guests

How to Save Money by Staying at a College This Summer:https://www.travelandleisure.com/travel-news/university-rooms-   college-dorms-summer-budget-accommodations

How to Stay at a College Residence Instead of a Hotel: https://traveltips.usatoday.com/stay-college-residence-instead-hotel- 10629.html

Summer Vacation on Campus: https://www.smithsonianmag.com/travel/summer-vacation-on-campus-111580874/

Rent a cabin

I haven't done this yet, so I don't have much expertise in this area, but I know of people who have rented a cabin for the weekend, a little retreat from hustle and bustle of the city and they loved the experience. There might be locations right in your state or surrounding states that have cabins. It could possibly be a short road trip to a perfect getaway. No need to pack fancy clothes or spend a lot going out to eat. Just grab some lounge pieces, board games, fill your cooler or with food to make sandwiches or to cook, grab that picnic basket and roll to the great outdoors and have fun. Do your research and be creative.

All Inclusive Family Resorts

A major cost associated with family travel is airfare and lodging. Once you've handled those pieces, meals and activities start to add up. That's where all-inclusive resorts come into play. There are many all-inclusive family resorts around the world, you just have to decide where you want to go and plan it out. I'm not an expert in this area, but I do know of a great resource with some cool ideas on all-inclusive family resorts whether in the Caribbean or Mexico and

beyond. Family Vacation Critic is the site to get great ideas on where to go and how to travel with a family. Check out their site at: https://www.familyvacationcritic.com/ideas/

Cruising with the Family

One of the most affordable vacations, which is essentially all-inclusive, is taking a cruise. Disney cruises are a bit more on the high-end side, but you can find more budget conscious cruises through lines like Carnival. Don't worry, they have plenty of safe and fun activities for children and teens. The bonus part is that you don't have to worry about finding a place to stay or food to eat because that is included in the cost of the trip. You can give your children a lifetime experience by traveling to various islands of the Caribbean. They will be able to learn about different cultures as well benefit from the whole travel experience.

Carnival Cruise Lines offers great deals from $149 pp (sometimes $99) if you select some off season or shorter trips, but with these prices, it makes travel much more affordable. So, let's say you have a family of four, $149 x 4 = $596 plus applicable taxes and fees. You could probably have a trip for under $800. It's possible, if you can put $133 per month together for 6 months or even a year ($1596) and have a very nice family vacation.

Maybe you cannot afford 4 -6 plane tickets right off hand, but if you can load up in a car or van and drive to the nearest port, then cruising will be a great option. Don't let anything stop you. If you choose to do so, always consider maximizing your trip. Maybe you can sail out of Miami/Ft. Lauderdale, or New Orleans. Try to get there a day earlier or schedule enough time to stay a day or two in the port area. Think about getting a suite with a kitchenette, grab some groceries and enjoy. One of my favorite hotel suites to stay at is *Home2 Suites by Hilton* https://home2suites3.hilton.com/en/index.html. The rooms are super huge, plus you have a kitchenette, a full or queen size sleeper sofa and you can get two queen beds. They also have a breakfast bar stocked with waffles, yogurt, cereal, breakfast sandwiches and a good selection of juices. Well, worth the price.

If you have children, you have students…so don't count out finding fares for student rates which will help to reduce expenses.

If you are looking to put together a cruise for your family and friends, check out the Travel Agent resources at the back of the book with dedicated and qualified agents that will ensure that you have the best cruise experience ever.

Save on Activities When Traveling to Popular U.S. Cities

One way to help plan out your family vacation and save in the process is to use e-commerce marketplaces such as Groupon (www.groupon.com).

Not only can you find great deals, but these sites offer a plethora of unique experiences so that you don't have to ponder much about what to do. Living Social www.livingsocial.com (acquired by Groupon) is the best place to find and share unique things to do in your area. With dozens of deal categories offering unforgettable local experiences, travel deals, products, and services in cities all over, we have everything you need to save money and explore your world.

Smart Destinations: Go City Card

https://www.smartdestinations.com/ - You can save up to 55% on top attractions, museums, tours & more. Do more & spend less with a *Go City Card*.

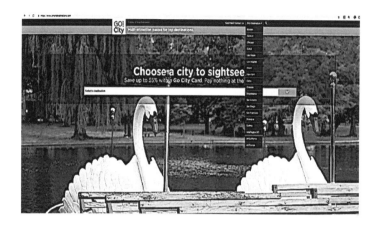

Sightseeing Pass: https://www.sightseeingpass.com/ Save Big on the Best Attractions with *The Sightseeing Pass*.

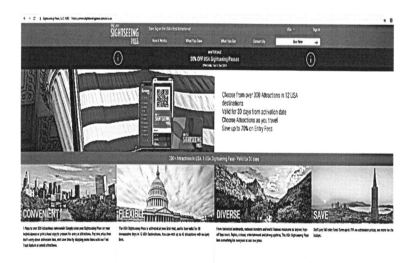

** Again, you can always go to Groupon and compare costs to see if you can get the Go Pass at a discount.

Example: **NYC Pass** allows you to choose from more than 75 tourist attractions. Some examples of what is offered is: Empire State Building, Top of the Rock, Hop-on Hop-off Bus, Statue of Liberty, Museum, Ice Skating, Radio City and much more

Here are a few more links for low-cost activities in some of the most popular

U.S. cities:

Chicago: https://www.choosechicago.com/things-to-do/free-and-cheap-things- to-do/

Los Angeles: https://www.discoverlosangeles.com/blog/100-almost-free-things- do-los-angeles

New York City: https://www.timeout.com/new-york-kids/things-to-do/free- things-to-do-with-kids-in-new-york. ** Look for the Red Booth in NY for half-priced Broadway tickets: https://www.nytix.com/broadway

Washington DC: https://washington.org/free-things-to-do and https://www.ytravelblog.com/free-cheap-things-to-do-washington-d-c/

Orlando: http://www.reserveorlando.com/travelguide/free-things-to-do-in- orlando-florida/ or https://orlandoonthecheap.com/25-orlando-attractions-under-30/

Dallas: https://www.visitdallas.com/things-to-do/trip-ideas/dallas-on-a-budget.html

One of my personal favorites is Timeout

https://www.timeout.com

Timeout is like the ultimate guide for finding things to do in any city worldwide. I first learned of Timeout when I was researching for my first trip to NYC. Not only was an online site available but I grabbed a guide while walking around NYC trying to find my way. This guide contains the best local attractions and entertainment along with listings of eateries. For your convenience, there is also a mobile app that you can download so that your guide can be at hand just in case you and your family find yourselves a little unsure as what to do next.

Another place to get excellent ideas and reviews is www.tripadvisor.com. You can search various cities, hotels, etc. and read the reviews to determine whether the decision you are considering is a wise one. If there are 100's of reviews, then you can rest assure it's pretty accurate. This site happens to be my go-to site whenever I am planning my travels. One of the great features is that they have forums that are quite active so if you have a question about something, I'm sure that you will receive a response within a day if now within a few hours.

Off the Beaten Path:

If you are taking a road trip, oftentimes as you are going down the highway, you will see signs that indicate there are various historic or scenic sites. On a road trip that I so vividly recall to St. Louis,

Mo, I passed a sign leading to Diamond, Missouri where George Washington Carver National Monument was located. I decided to stop and am so glad that I did. It was one of the best decisions that I had made on my journey. So much rich history and inspiration.

That's just an example, but there are many others along the way. I hope that you will give your children the experience of a true history lesson on the road.

Planning and Savings Tip: Go through the various online travel guides such as www.timeout.com or www.tripadvisor.com and pick out a few activities that you are interested in. Do a search on www.groupon.com and see if you can grab a deal, if so you've saved your family from having to pay full price. Enjoy yourselves!

Cool Places to Go If You Have Children Under 12
(some are even for the young at heart):

Disney! Yes, that's always a plus but wait, there's more.

 Legoland - Winterhaven, FL

Universal Studios - This is a must! Heck, you don't have to be 12 and under to enjoy this experience. It's great for those in the 29, 39, 49, 59, 69 plus club!!! Knott's Berry Farm - Buena Park, California

Busch Gardens - Williamsburg, VA

Seaworld - Orlando, Florida; San Diego,California;
San Antonio, Texas

Silver Dollar City - Branson, Mo

Johnson Space Center - Houston, Texas

Science Museum - Oklahoma City

Schlitterbahn Waterpark - New Braunfels, Texas (there are different locations all around, but the original location is a must) - Definitely fun for the youth and young at heart! This location has two waterparks. Also, while in New Braunfels you might want to take an extra day out from the waterpark and go tubing (float) down the river. It's popular family activity.

Great Wolf Lodge Waterpark - Grapevine, Texas; Kansas City, Kansas; Grand Mound, Washington

More family vacation resources:

25 Coolest Family Vacation Spots in the U.S.:
https://www.gobankingrates.com/saving-money/travel/best-family-vacation-spots-in-us/#20

Family Travel Blogs that will inspire you to hit to road by Red Tricycle Blog: http://redtri.com/top-family-travel-blogs/

Kids Fly Free? Discount Fares for Children

Frontier Airlines o☐ers a yearly subscription option known as Discount Den☐ (https://www.flyfrontier.com/deals/discount-den/). It allows you to have exclusive access to Frontier's lowest available fares (DEN DEALS) across their routes all year long. For the first year, the fee is $59.99 and then $59.99 for every subsequent year. The lower fares are available for up to 6 people on your itinerary, as long as you are one of the passengers.

If you plan on taking a train ride across the country, Amtrak (https://www.amtrak.com/children-discounts) offers a 50% discount off of an adult fare for children from ages 2 to 11.

Student Fares and Travel Discounts

These sites are great for helping to plan family vacation with students or even if you have a teen or young adult in college that is has activities such as band/choir competitions, exchange students or studying abroad, these are options are great to check out as well.

Student Universe - studentuniverse.com - We offer exclusive student flight discounts that can't be found anywhere else and offer steeper flight and travel deals when we know students want to travel.

STA Travel - http://www.statravel.com - The world's largest student and youth travel company

Spring Break deals for students: https://onmogul.com/stories/how-to-spring- break-without-breaking-the-bank

Make Memories!

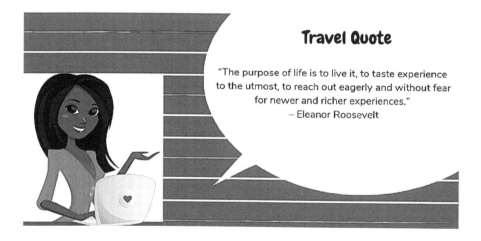

Travel Quote

"The purpose of life is to live it, to taste experience to the utmost, to reach out eagerly and without fear for newer and richer experiences."
– Eleanor Roosevelt

Couples

Oh Darling, Let's Be Adventurers

This book is just an extension of wanting to see families, especially married couples, make time for another amidst all of the responsibilities and demands of life. It is with great pleasure to be able to help spark some ideas and eliminate some of the factors that may prevent you from taking the time out to get away with the one you love.

"I would like to travel the world with you twice. Once to see the world. Twice, to see the way you see the world."
– Anonymous

The Power of Disconnect to Reconnect

How often do you and your spouse travel together? Not for "me" time, but for "we" time. A getaway is a time to bond, to play, to rekindle the flame and go back to the center of which brought both of you together in the first place. It should be a time to look forward to once or twice a year. No children, no work, no social media...just the two of you. Even if you decide to make a couple's trip with some of your closest married friends, then invite them so that there can be a little balance, but make sure you get some alone time in as well.

Below is an infographic by Travelocity that gives some statistics on Romance by the Numbers and the most popular cities couples go to for a romantic getaway. This may only be a small representation of the total population but still something to think about.

Planning Together

When planning a trip with your significant other, you must take into consideration that it is a team effort and something that should include the interests of both parties, even if you are planning a trip as a surprise. You could start by hinting on some thoughts to get an idea of what the other person would love to do.

If it is your first time going on a couples' trip since your honeymoon, then start with a small getaway, maybe over a weekend.

Here are a few tips for planning:

- Have activities planned
- Get suggestions from others who have traveled to the desired location
- Consider a great travel agent (One who has a passion for helping others experience the best and most rewarding vacation ever and who has some great travel experiences of their own)
- Be spontaneous and open to Plan B if your original plans fall through
- Make the most of your trip and have fun with one another

Honey Moon Ideas

On a tight budget but want to have a nice honeymoon? Maybe you had to bank the honeymoon until a later time but you really want to celebrate that glorious occasion. Please remember, at the end of the day, the union and purpose are the most important thing ever. However, you've been together a year or a little longer and you still desire to have your dream vacation/honeymoon. Well, it's never too late and I can point you in the direction to some great options on where to go and how to get started.

Honeyfund.com - If you are in the pre-planning phases of your wedding or you would like to do something for a special anniversary and desire your closest family and friends to sow into your dream, then Honey Fund is a great option. Honeyfund.com is the free honeymoon registry and #1 cash wedding gift registry. The fun part is that you get to select the type of honeymoon you desire, choose a destination and then you can set up your dream vacation and itemize your expenses (i.e. airfare, hotel, excursions, etc.) and set small increments for people to chip into to meet the goal.

What's Your Dream Honeymoon Destination?

When signing up with Honey Fund, you will also receive travel deals which is a bonus of the service.

It is estimated that a couple can spend between $4000 - $5000 on a honeymoon but maybe you only have half of that, approximately $2500. Check out the scenario below. I used the wherefor.com site and entered a budget of $2500 for two people for 5 days. Now I know international travel and vacationing may not be all that conducive to time, but at least you know there are options. Besides, if you want to take the risk of vacationing for 3 days for the international experience, then what is holding you back? Oh, the places you can go!! (Later in this book, I will also show you how to save effortlessly)

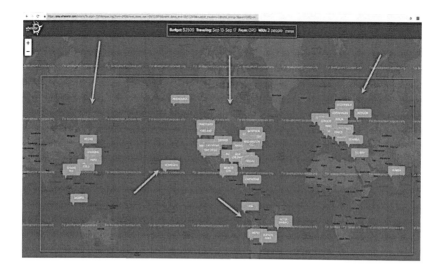

If you are looking to do a little something different than the traditional hotel stay while traveling with your significant other internationally, consider renting a villa.

The Villas of Distinction website:
(https://www.villasofdistinction.com) explains the uniqueness and value of a villa:

Villas are luxurious, private residences that are made available to vacation travelers. Villas usually range from 1-20 bedrooms and offer additional living spaces: living rooms, dining rooms, fully-equipped kitchens, and outdoor areas including verandas and pools. They are usually equipped with amenities and a dedicated staff to cater to your specific needs. Luxury villas are often more economical for traveling families and couples.

Why rent a villa over a hotel or resort?

•	Personalized attention and service from an experienced Villa Specialist and Concierge

•	Allows you to create a unique, customized experience based on your needs

• Superb value – spend less, receive more; villas are often a much better value per person than hotels or resort suites

• Complete privacy – you have complete space by yourself

• Great for all occasions, from big group gatherings to intimate getaways

• Many different options – choose from thousands of villas in over 50 destinations across the globe

• Not a timeshare or fractional ownership – travel where you want, when you want, without membership fees

Here are some other sites to check out to rent villas:

https://www.rentavilla.com

https://www.rentvillas.com

Timeshares without memberships

I'm sure that you received a phone call or two or have come across some type of promotion for a trip with a set number of days for an extremely low cost, like pennies to the dollar. Now I cannot tell you to jump on any blind deal from a random phone call or flyer, so you might do some checking around to see if this could be an option for your vacation. I've been on a trip where there was a 90-minute presentation without a whole deal of pressure to buy a timeshare.

However, I do know that you can use sites like VRBO.com to actually rent a timeshare from an owner or other really nice lodging choices, such as this private suite mansion nestled in the luscious land of the State of Georgia. This was at a whopping rate of $76 per night.

Have a little fun in the sun

How about a beach location? The kind that you can wake up and literally open your balcony doors to the fresh breeze of the ocean or only a few feet away from the beach that you can go for a sunrise or sunset walk. I actually expanded my search a bit by going to www.vacationrenter.com which is a website aggregator for vacation rentals.

What's pretty cool about Vacation Renter is that if will show you a price map of the various rentals in your chosen area. From my search, I found a beach front bijou studio with a price range of about $113 per night, which isn't bad at all. Plus, the reviews were pretty high.

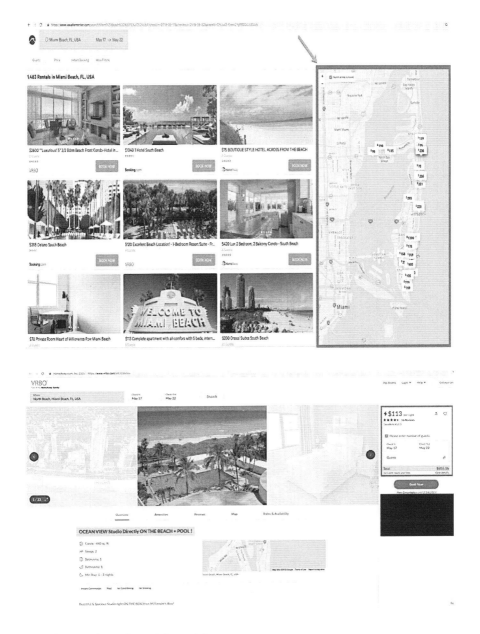

Traditional Bed and Breakfast

Traditional Bed and Breakfast locations are privately owned residences with sleeping accommodations and a morning breakfast. Bed and Breakfast Inns are private with a personalized touch.

Article from U.S. News: https://travel.usnews.com/gallery/30-charming-bed-and-breakfasts-across-america

SecretPlaces.com - Secret places is an independent guide to some of the most beautiful and authentic hotels, bed and breakfast, and holiday homes in Europe and beyond.

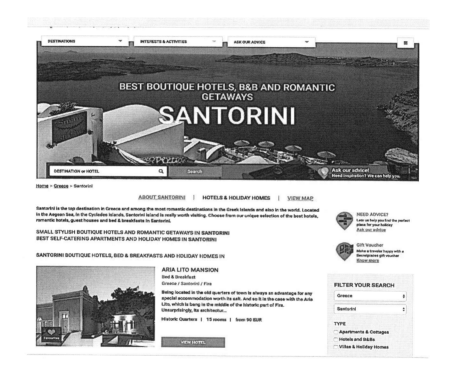

Rent a Private Island

Yes, you read it correctly!

Start here -> Google: "Private Islands for rent"

If you want to be super impressive, you can rent Necker Island owned by Virgin Atlantic founder, Richard Branson though it would only cost you a whopping $42,000 per night, but if you have it like that then by all means be their guest.

While some of these options might be out of your price range or what you are willing to spend, you may be more surprised that there are plenty that are budget friendly. This may be an excellent time to grab a few of your friends and their significant others and split the cost. In fact, you might be able to get a flat rate per night and after everyone puts in their parts, it will be quite affordable.

I can't caution enough, regardless wherever you stay, make sure to do plenty of research about the area and place you choose to stay. Even though it might be a remote/private island, make sure that you have a plan in case of an emergency.

All Inclusive Resorts and Adult Only Resorts/Hotels

Most of you have heard of Beaches and Sandals, both are all-inclusive resorts planted in beautiful locations in the Caribbean and beyond, but they can be a bit pricey. There is a way to put together an affordable getaway without cutting out all of the perks luxuries of a nice vacation stay. Maybe you want to stay at an all-inclusive resort that includes meals and activities which may cost a little more but it may balance out if you can catch an airfare deal. I think they key is to be as flexible as possible.

While planning your trip out for the year, you could set different time frames, so let's say your desired month of travel is March, but June and September are open. whether months or days within a month and travel on some of the odd days like a Tuesday or Thursday and return the following Tuesday or Thursday, if you have the time.

Sites like www.iberostar.com offer a selection of all-inclusive adult only resorts in Mexico and Jamaica.

Boutique Hotels

What is a boutique hotel and why would it be great for couples?

A boutique hotel is smaller than a conventional hotel, usually having less than 100 rooms with a touch of sophistication and luxury. It's generally located within an urban setting. Some are branched from larger chains but are known to be part of their collection while a vast majority of them are independently owned. Guests often received a more personalized touch and service. Boutique hotels are catered toward adults or business professionals.

Tablet Hotels www.tablethotels.com - The best boutique & luxury hotels with verified hotel reviews, dependable customer service & the best rates guaranteed.

Take for example, you want to spend two or three nights in Miami, by using the Tablet Hotels website or app, you can find They also use a feature called Site Compare to guarantee that you are getting the lowest price available. I also took it a step further and used TripAdvisor to check the ratings and prices and the hotel Tablet is suggesting is highly rated. However, TripAdvisor shows even more of a rate reduction for the same dates.

In this case, you may be able to go back to Tablet and tell them that you were able to find a lower rate and see if they will match it. It really all depends on how much you want to save and in doing so, it may require a little research before locking in prices. Don't overdo it but keep your eyes open.

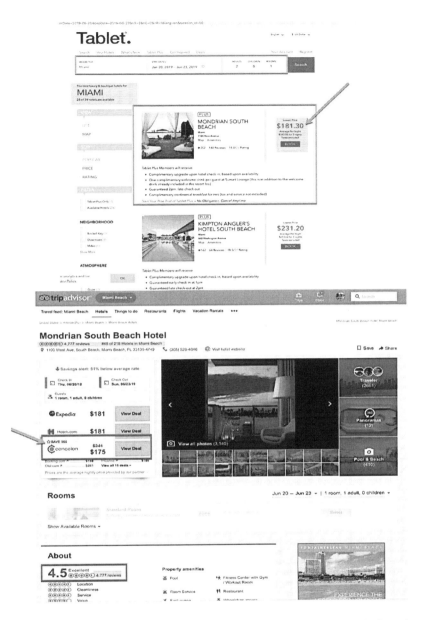

Another site that compiles an array of boutique hotel is The Guestbook https://theguestbook.com. However, what makes The Guestbook unique and appealing is that you can get cashback or trip cash on bookings through the site. All you have to do is book your room directly with a member hotel through their site or theguestbook.com and earn 5% cash back through PayPal, gift cards, charitable donation, or double your reward as 10% Trip Cash but that cash back could go into your savings fund for your next trip.

How to save up for your vacation?

This is the fun part. Oftentimes, saving for your vacation is one of the biggest barriers if not the greatest in your planning process. Now this concept is nothing new, so I may be presenting the method to some and introducing it to others. The best part about this plan is you can use this for practically any financial goal. Not only can you use this method for travel goals but it can be applied to general savings goals, creating an emergency fund, debt elimination strategies, down payments, business ventures and investments and so on - It Is Possible!

Hopefully this will inspire you to do so. If you google, 52-week savings challenge or 26-week savings challenge you will find templates and trackers to use. The general idea of the challenge is to create a goal and this method will help you to save per day, week, or month for a specific time period. What's so simple about it is depending on your savings goal, you really won't miss the money because you can save in small increments and the milestones are set for you.

Create what works for you as a couple. In fact, if you both are chipping in, let's say $2500 per person, then the combined goal would be $5000. Each of you will be responsible to put in your part but at the end of the period you will have reached your maximum amount, if not more. Make it fun.

You can even download an app such as the *52 Week Money Savings Challenge* app: https://apps.romerock.com/52-weeks-money-savings-challenge/

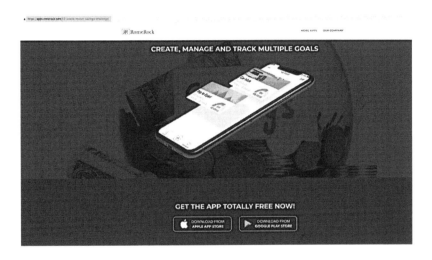

Here's a template for you to use to manually track your weekly savings using the 52-week savings challenge method. All you have to do is deposit (save) the dollar amount according to the week. At the end of the 52 weeks, you will have saved $1378.00. You can do this with family members, friends, or groups.

Date	Week	Deposit Amt	Savings Bal	Complete	Date	Week	Deposit Amt	Savings Bal	Complete
	1	$ 1.00	$ 1.00			27	$ 27.00	$ 378.00	
	2	$ 2.00	$ 3.00			28	$ 28.00	$ 406.00	
	3	$ 3.00	$ 6.00			29	$ 29.00	$ 435.00	
	4	$ 4.00	$ 10.00			30	$ 30.00	$ 465.00	
	5	$ 5.00	$ 15.00			31	$ 31.00	$ 496.00	
	6	$ 6.00	$ 21.00			32	$ 32.00	$ 528.00	
	7	$ 7.00	$ 28.00			33	$ 33.00	$ 561.00	
	8	$ 8.00	$ 36.00			34	$ 34.00	$ 595.00	
	9	$ 9.00	$ 45.00			35	$ 35.00	$ 630.00	
	10	$ 10.00	$ 55.00			36	$ 36.00	$ 666.00	
	11	$ 11.00	$ 66.00			37	$ 37.00	$ 703.00	
	12	$ 12.00	$ 78.00			38	$ 38.00	$ 741.00	
	13	$ 13.00	$ 91.00			39	$ 39.00	$ 780.00	
	14	$ 14.00	$ 105.00			40	$ 40.00	$ 820.00	
	15	$ 15.00	$ 120.00			41	$ 41.00	$ 861.00	
	16	$ 16.00	$ 136.00			42	$ 42.00	$ 903.00	
	17	$ 17.00	$ 153.00			43	$ 43.00	$ 946.00	
	18	$ 18.00	$ 171.00			44	$ 44.00	$ 990.00	
	19	$ 19.00	$ 190.00			45	$ 45.00	$ 1,035.00	
	20	$ 20.00	$ 210.00			46	$ 46.00	$ 1,081.00	
	21	$ 21.00	$ 231.00			47	$ 47.00	$ 1,128.00	
	22	$ 22.00	$ 253.00			48	$ 48.00	$ 1,176.00	
	23	$ 23.00	$ 276.00			49	$ 49.00	$ 1,225.00	
	24	$ 24.00	$ 300.00			50	$ 50.00	$ 1,275.00	
	25	$ 25.00	$ 325.00			51	$ 51.00	$ 1,326.00	
	26	$ 26.00	$ 351.00			52	$ 52.00	$ 1,378.00	

6 Month Savings Plan:

Time Frame	Combined	Per Person
6 Months	$5000	$2500
Monthly (4 weeks)	$833.34	$416.68
Weekly	$208.34	$104.17

*** Please know that there are many ways to save a specific amount per week, per month, per year. This is just an example of how two people can work together to save toward their travel goals in a short period of time. ***

13 Week Savings Matrix

The 13-week savings matrix is something that I created for a rapid and short-term savings plan. It shows how many dollars you would save a day or specific days of the week ending in a total sum of $4186 in just a little over 3 months. The special part about this matrix is that you can save according to the number of Sunday's etc. in a 13-week period (vertically), or per week (horizontally). You can basically make your end goal to meet your needs. All you have to do is save according to the number in the space for that time period. * The power of compounding. *

Week	Sun	M	T	W	Th	F	Sat	Week Ending Savings
1	1	2	3	4	5	6	7	28
2	8	9	10	11	12	13	14	77
3	15	16	17	18	19	20	21	126
4	22	23	24	25	26	27	28	175
5	29	30	31	32	33	34	35	224
6	36	37	38	39	40	41	42	273
7	43	44	45	46	47	48	49	322
8	50	51	52	53	54	55	56	371
9	57	58	59	60	61	62	63	420
10	64	65	66	67	68	69	70	469
11	71	72	73	74	75	76	77	518
12	78	79	80	81	82	83	84	567
13	85	86	87	88	89	90	91	616
Per weekday within 13 weeks	559	572	585	598	611	624	637	4186
							Total 13-week Savings Matrix	4186

Twine App - is a savings and investment app for couples. It can be used to for various type of goals such as saving for a home, business ventures, as an investment strategy, a vacation or honeymoon and much more. All you have to do is set a goal and set up the method for how you will fund the account. The best part is that both of you can contribute to the goal and watch it grow. Once you've reached your milestone, it's time to get ready to celebrate!!

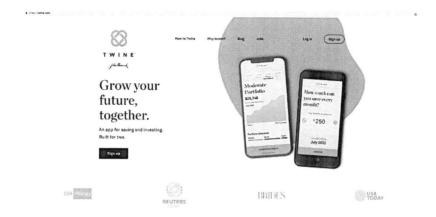

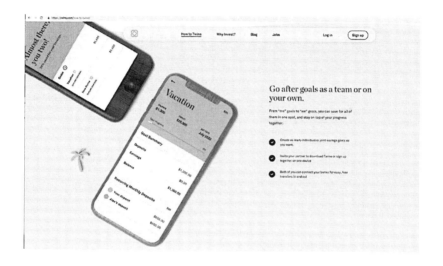

This is just a sample of ideas to get your creative juices flowing in order to create the perfect getaway for (or with) the one you love.

Sites to use: Wherefor.com, Google Flights, www.Expedia.com, Roomkey.com and TripAdvisor.com

* For selected hotels, check Tripadvisor.com reviews to ensure that it is a good choice. If you have some wiggle room in your budget upgrade to a 5-star establishment. You can use this site to find a great deal, search around a bit more or use it to purchase a flight and option out for alternative lodging if it will keep you under budget.

I've created 3 example getaways using Wherefor.com and included how to check reviews of the suggested hotel on Trip Advisor. Please keep in mind, prices vary.

** Sample departure cities are used so prices may vary.

USA Getaway
Destination: NYC
Nice Weekend Getaway - 4 days, 3 nights
Budget: $1500

The site returns possible locations to go with the specified budget. In this example, this couple will be going to NYC from Phoenix, Arizona.

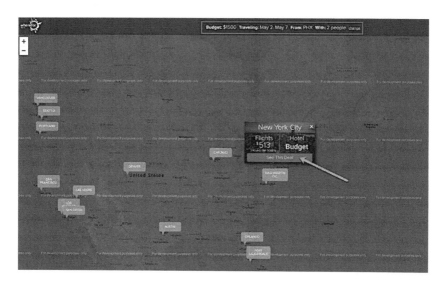

This selection includes flight and hotel for about $650 over the budget, however the flight is a decent deal give or take. This is your decision to pick and choose whether you want to get a better rate piecing it together. You can use Google Flights. For hotels you can search Google Expedia and Trip Advisor to broaden your scope.

In this example, the suggested hotel is Sheraton Tribeca New York. Though it is a nice location and a great hotel, I really want to stay closer to the budget as well as find a setting which will create more of a romantic feel in *The City That Never Sleeps* after all, this is a supposed to be a romantic getaway. I decided to search for a hotel that was still relatively affordable and chic but with a trendy vibe.

By using Google Flights, I was able to capture fares a few dollars lower that Wherefor's suggested prices. To better gauge prices, I used the price graph and looked for the lowest indicator that fit a great date range. In this case, the total cost per person is $228.39 or $456.78 altogether, which is about a $56 savings from Wherefor.

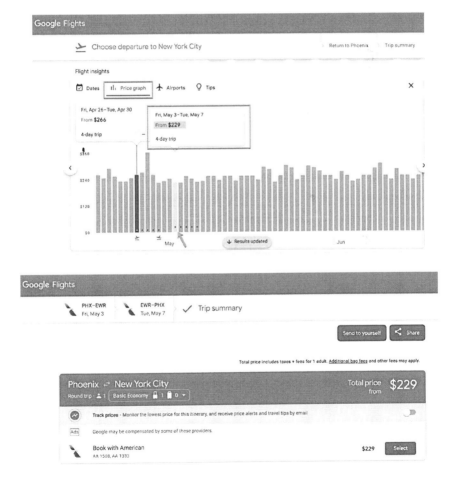

Now that we have the airfare out of the way, it's time to select a hotel that meets our criteria. There is a little over $1000 left in the budget. The following choices were a over the budget by $100 - 500, however this is because it is based on location, amenities, and general ambiance. The Marcel at Gramercy, a local boutique hotel nestled in the Gramercy neighborhood and an easy walk to some of the most popular neighborhoods: Gramercy Park, East Village, Chelsea, and SoHo. The Marcel amounted to $1162.65 for the total stay. The other option is Millennium Broadway New York which is located in the heart of Times Square. For this hotel, I selected the Millennium Suite with a view of Times Square and the total amount is $1452.

** Of course, there are cheaper lodging options that you can consider when going to New York City, such as staying in New Jersey and taking the train over or retreating to a less "touristy" district where the rates will be significantly lower. Besides, NYC is a place where it's easy to get around. It's all in what you are looking for and what your budget can accommodate.

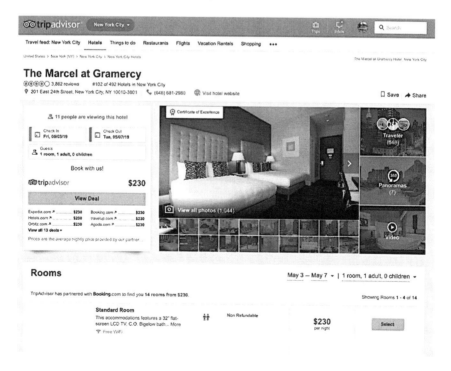

SUPERIOR ROOM W/KING BED

SCROLL DOWN

The Marcel at Gramercy

Guests Love It Because of...

💬 **"Great Location"**
99 related reviews

💬 **"Great Parking"**
19 related reviews

1 Room: Standard Room

Check-in: May 3, 2019
Check-out: May 7, 2019
4-night stay
Save 30%

Your price summary

	avg./night
Room 1: 2 Adults	
4 Nights ⌄	$230.30
Taxes per night	$37.46
Total due today: $1,071.05	
Due at Property: ⌃	$91.60
Resort fee	$91.60

Room Total: $1,162.65

Rates are quoted in **US dollars**. Taxes and Fees due at the property are based on current exchange rates, and are payable in local currency.

149

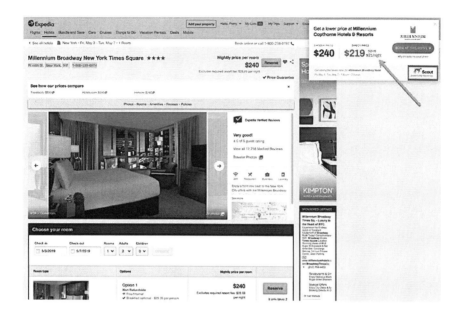

Island Getaway

Destination: Punta Cana, Dominican Republic
Extended Weekend Getaway - 5 days, 4 nights
Budget: $3500

In this example, I used Google Flights to find the airfare for
$1402.26 in total for 2 passengers.

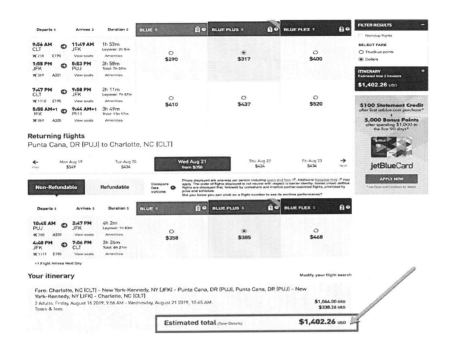

For the lodging arrangements, I chose to go with VRBO.com and select an option with the highest ratings and the most reviews, both are important factors. I was able to find a beautiful condo on the beach for $749 total which made this awesome weekend getaway approximately $1350 under budget.

European Getaway

Destination: Venice (ex. 7 days from Houston, Texas)
Budget: $5000

For this scenario, I used Google Flights again and was able to capture a phenomenal rate for 2 people traveling from Houston, TX to Venice, Italy for $1380.14, leaving approximately $3600 for lodging and extra. I think it is fair to say that you could either stay at a traditional hotel or a more private option.

Below is a snapshot of hotel options using Expedia.com and Villa options using VRBO.com. We were able to capture 7 nights at Hotel Moresco, the top-rated hotel in Venice for $2005.93, leaving a surplus of approximately $1600 to wine and dine. The second option is called The Molino Apartment located in St. Mark's Square and only costs $1050.53 for all 7 nights leaving approximately $2500 in the bank. These are definitely great options and well under budget.

Hotel Moresco

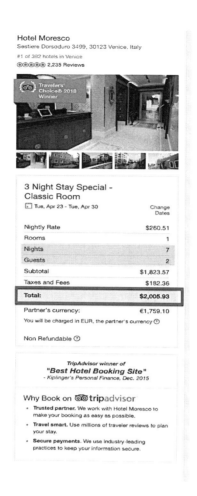

Hotel Moresco

Sestiere Dorsoduro 3499, 30123 Venice, Italy

#1 of 392 hotels in Venice

⊚⊚⊚⊚⊚ 2,235 Reviews

Travelers' Choice® 2018 Winner

3 Night Stay Special - Classic Room

Tue, Apr 23 - Tue, Apr 30   Change Dates

Nightly Rate	$260.51
Rooms	1
Nights	7
Guests	2
Subtotal	$1,823.57
Taxes and Fees	$182.36
Total:	**$2,005.93**

Partner's currency: €1,759.10

You will be charged in EUR, the partner's currency ⑦

Non Refundable ⑦

TripAdvisor winner of
"Best Hotel Booking Site"
- *Kiplinger's Personal Finance, Dec. 2015*

Why Book on ⊚⊚ tripadvisor

- **Trusted partner.** We work with Hotel Moresco to make your booking as easy as possible.
- **Travel smart.** Use millions of traveler reviews to plan your stay.
- **Secure payments.** We use industry-leading practices to keep your information secure.

Option 2:

Travel Tours:

If you all don't want to deal with the details of planning a vacation and you have a budget and location in mind, then taking a travel tour just might be a great option. This may also take the edge off of deciding on what to do

Let's take it up a Notch...Living the Yacht Life...

Traditional Cruise? How about taking it up a notch by having your own private chartered yacht or catamaran? Don't think that it is possible or too expensive? Then, think again. Most options allow you to sail on your own, but if you don't have sailing experience or want more of a concierge type experience with a crewed charter with a captain or add on a private skipper and your own chef.

While this may be a little pricier than expected, don't you think that you both deserve a great time away? Maybe, spend three days at sea and a couple of days on shore. Imagine, the two of you enjoying the beauty of the Caribbean or the most glorious views of the sovereign land of the Greek isles, by creating your own nautical experience. Even though this could be a private couple vacation, it wouldn't hurt to invite some of your closest couple friends to join in.

These ideas may be a little more on the high end but it depends on your individual budget and how you are able to cut costs in other areas, such as airfare.

Example: Maybe you and your spouse have set aside $5000 to spend on a nice week vacation getaway, then the options below are deemed to fit your budget. One thing to keep in mind on these sites is to check for specials as well as check out for times during an off season. These types of cruises have lengths of 5 days or more.

The Moorings offers travelers a unique way to explore the islands and experience the thrill of sailing.

20+
Destinations
Worldwide

5-Star Sailing
Experiences

Loyalty
Rewards
Program

Full Service
Travel
Assistance

Award
Winning
Catamarans

Tradition of
Excellence

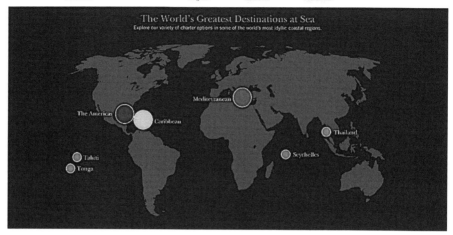

Here are some sample bookings from www.moorings.com:
7 nights with 6 passengers ($513.00 per person)

Home · Destinations · Mediterranean · Greece · Athens Zea

Athens Zea Yacht Charter

Build My Quote   Itinerary   Cruising Conditions   Travel Notes

From Price
$3,080
Yacht price & fees

Sailing ›	edit
Sat 28 Sep 2019 ›	edit
6 Passengers ›	edit
7 nights ›	edit

Moorings 45 - 3 Cabin Monohull   edit

| 3 Cabins | 45'9" ft | 1-3 yrs old | 8 People |

Continue

Email Quote

Save your quotes for later

Overview

If you are seeking an offshore vacation that's packed with terrific conditions, beautiful landscapes, historically significant ancient ruins, secluded islands, vibrant nightlife, a warm culture and terrific cuisine – Greece is the place to be.

Located on the southern end of mainland Greece, Marina Zea is perfectly situated for an exhilarating yacht charter vacation through the wondrous Saronic Gulf. This cruising ground provides travelers with a wealth of opportunities to experience Grecian culture through ancient ruins, towering landscapes, decadent cuisine and

Additional chartered yacht companies:

BoatsAtSea.com - Their portfolio offers more than 1100 crewed charter yachts with professional crews cater to all your wishes. Whether you prefer a small sailing boat, comfortable catamaran, or luxurious motor yacht.

Antlos.com is like the Airbnb of boat rental. Antlos is a peer-to-peer service that allows skippers and captains to directly list their boat on the site and set a price per person per night, which includes the skipper and boat rental.

Click&Boat https://www.clickandboat.com/us is a peer to peer network that offers you the chance to charter yachts, sailboats, motorboats, RIBs, barges, catamarans and jet skis.
www.windstarcruises.com

These are not the only sites out there, but at least this gives you a good idea as to what is available. In fact, depending on the location that you travel to such as Florida or California and various locations overseas, there are local rental services.

Seasonal Travel:

You probably hear a lot about traveling in off-seasons but may not be too clear as to what months actually constitute a particular season. Here is a reference below:

Peak season (roughly mid-June through August),

Shoulder season (April through mid-June and September through October)
Off season (November through March)

The reason why off seasons are the close to perfect times to travel is because most people travel during the Peak and Shoulder seasons. Typically, Spring through early Fall, although a lot of people travel during the major holidays that do fall in the off seasons (Thanksgiving, Christmas, and New Year's). Things like the weather, the possibility that certain attractions could be closed, as well as travel conditions could be adding to the discouragement of travel. The benefit of traveling during these times could mean small crowds and greater deals.

Get Hyped Up About It!

Do things that will keep you motivated. Create a vision board. Study the destination, find things to do, places to each, connect with various travel groups online - like Facebook Travel groups and ask plenty of questions. You can even download a countdown tracker such as the one below. You can find one in your mobile app store, just download and get to counting down.

Whatever you choose to do, make it a priority to set time aside and take a nice getaway with your significant other. Quality time is everything. Bon Voyage!

Solo Travelers

Quote for Thought

"You can never cross the ocean until you have the courage to lose sight of the shore."
– Christopher Columbus

How I broke the cycle of holding myself back from living life?

Hint: I did it solo!

A little background about how I started my travel journey. Back in 2002, I moved back to my hometown and after a year of being home, I realized that I needed a change of scenery. That's what keeps me motivated, especially after living in and visiting larger cities that had a bit more to offer. I remember it was about a week out and I was looking at a map for places that I had never had been to and decided to go to New York City. It was totally on a whim! At the time, my budget was extremely limited and I was looking for an affordable way to make this dream happen. I searched high and low, looked at airplane tickets and got a bit discouraged because I had waited until the last minute so ticket prices were unbearably high especially flying from my city. I decided to try Amtrak. Sure, it was going to be a longer journey, but I was able to see parts of the country as well as meet interesting people along my journey that I would have never seen or met had I not taken this path. Plus, as the trip went on, I realized that my fear of "going solo" was slowly dissipating.

From there, I booked with Amtrak and then the next task was to find a place to stay. I had always heard that New York City with a very expensive place to visit let alone trying to find a decent place to lodge without breaking the bank. So, I decided to try an unconventional method. I decided to search Craigslist. Yes, I said Craigslist! This was before the days of Airbnb and other alternative lodging startups were born. Craigslist was a bit safer than it is today. I can't say I would try that method now but it worked for me then and I don't regret it one bit.

I looked day in and day out and there were options that caught my interest but I was a little leery. What if these people are crazy? What if I get there and this post was fake and I'm stuck in this big city all by myself? Well, trust me, I had questions but in the back of my mind, but with every question, I had a backup plan. Trust me!

It wasn't until this Bed and Breakfast host had messaged me personally and asked me if I was still looking for a place to stay. I was a little taken back that she knew that I was looking but I think that I had placed a post of 'in search of' and then deleted it a day or two later. I inquired a bit more as to what she had to offer and negotiated on that offer. Remember, I had a tight budget and it worked for her because she just needed to find someone to fill the open spot so that she was able to meet her weekly occupancy goal. Much to my surprise, I found out that she had a very nice Brownstone in Brooklyn in which she hosted several travelers at a time.

I performed extensive background research and finally made peace with my decision. She had given me her information so that we could talk directly by phone and she reached out to me all the way until it was time for me to board the train and start my journey. It was the best decision I could have ever made for my first real solo trip. I stayed in New York City for about seven days and paid in under $500 for the whole trip excluding my meals, entertainment, and some small souvenirs. You might be thinking what in the world could you get in New York for $500 but let me tell you, it is possible! That's when I made up my mind that I would do the proper research before making final plans on a trip. I realized that it's not as hard as we think it is but it does take a little time and proper planning to make it all happen.

Was I lonely traveling by myself?

Absolutely not but don't get me wrong, there were moments when it would have been nice for someone to share the experience with but once I started to take in all the culture and activities that NYC had to offer, all that went away. Besides, it's really not too difficult to make friends along the way. These weren't the kind of friends that you would tell them where you stay but the ones who might be in a general area. For example, I'd get up early each morning and walk to the train station but on my way, I would stop in this little convenient store to get some little snacks and would always make small talk with the cashier. He was one of very, very few that knew that I was not from NYC but he told me about a little breakfast spot around the corner from the store. By the way, they had a full breakfast with pancakes, eggs, and sausage with orange juice for about $3.00. No joke! (The second time I went to NYC, I found a lot of little spots with a full breakfast under $5). He asked me if I knew P. Diddy (Sean Combs) and commenced to telling me that his restaurant, Junior's, was a block or two away as well.

On another occasion, I happened to get up in the wee hours of the morning to get to Times Square to see *Good Morning America* live. I wanted a front row standing space so I had to be there quite early. Before I got there, I stopped by my favorite little convenient store and asked my buddy if he had something that I could make a sign with because I was headed to the show. I needed a sign!! He found me a large neon orange poster board and I bought some little metallic stars that they used to use in grade school. I quickly created my sign that simply read "HI" and rushed to the area. There were already people standing out there when I had arrived but I was able to get a front row spot leaning on the little fence. Guess what? Al Roker walked straight up to me and greeted me. How's that? While I was standing there, this lady had asked if I was from there and if I was by myself. I was a little apprehensive in telling her at first, but I whispered to her "No, but I don't want anyone to know that". Well, except her, I guess. I had asked her if she was visiting (obviously so, because it was a weekday and both of us were in Time Square at a time most people would either be getting ready for work or at work) and she told me that she was here for the first time with her husband, but he was there on business which left her by herself. She asked me if I wanted to grab some lunch and I felt comfortable enough to go. We both were clueless so we just started walking until we found a restaurant. We had a great conversation and we ended up spending the whole day together. It was the best experience ever. We visited the Observatory at the Empire State Building and I had some VIP tickets to go back to visit a live taping of *The View*. She was in amazement. We really had the best time.

There is so much that I could share with you about making friends along the way but hopefully you can see how it you don't have to necessarily be by yourself. Be aware and don't share too much information but be open a little. If you don't feel peace, then keep it moving.

There are perks to solo travel

I've found that you might receive preferential treatment while traveling by yourself especially when attending events. Maybe because it's only one of you and they need to fill a seat or only have one spot available. Why not be a seat filler? That happened to me when attending on of the live tapings of *The View*. I happened to be standing in line and they were counting off the number of people per party and I was a party of one. The organizer picked me out and asked me to follow her. I was just excited to be in the studio. She walked me around the front and sat me right dab in the center of the set. I could literally take a few steps and hop of on the platform to join them at the table, though I don't think that would have been a wise idea. I just remember looking at Barbara Walters in the face like wow, this is crazy. To add amazement, it was either Barbara Walters or Joy Behar that had asked someone in the audience a question, which happened to be their Executive Producer at the time. His name was Bill Geddie which dawned on me in a split second because my mom would always talk about him and what happened on the show. The thing that through me off is he answered and I realized that he was sitting right next to me and the camera was on spot in my face. I tried to smile and look excited but I was still in utter amazement. My mom and a few other people were able to see me on live tv that day. After the show, grabbed my camera so I could pose in the set and she took me back in the back (just me) to see the Green Room. How cool is that? Being solo, a smile, and patience played a factor.

You only spent $500 on the total trip to NYC?

What did you do for fun?

The best way I can answer this and I think you will get the gist throughout this book is that I did quite a bit of research. If you travel to a large city, which I would suggest for solo travelers, there is bound to be a number of fun, free or discounted activities to do. Since it was NYC, I knew that there were many live talk shows taped there so I looked up how to get tickets to attend them. Some are required to get way in advance of about 6 months or more, while others have about a week wait time. You can get tickets from a couple of ways: 1. Through the company website (but you might have conducted a deep search to find the option, such as on abc.com website. From the homepage, scroll to the bottom of the page and select Company Information, then it will return all the other options. 2. Another way is to use affiliate sites that allows you to choose any Live TV Audience events available in the are you are visiting. If you ever visit a city where they have a live studio audience please try to go. It is one of the best experiences and you get to really see the dynamics of how things are shown on tv versus how it really is.

Here's the actual link to ABC's TV Ticket Request:
https://abc.go.com/tv-ticket-request

NBC's Ticket Request link is also located at the bottom of their homepage:

One of my favorite guides that they offer in NYC in the magazine/literature bins or online is Time Out Magazine. In fact, Time Out Magazine covers various cities around the world and it is a must have in your travel stash. They offer a listing to the shows and ticket information. Here's an example of the one for NYC: https://www.timeout.com/newyork/things-to-do/best-tv-show-tapings-in-nyc.

On Camera Audiences: http://on-camera-audiences.com/
TvTickets.com: http://www.tvtickets.com/

Go City Card and City Pass:

Another great option for affordable things to do is using the Go City Card by Smart Destinations (https://www.smartdestinations.com/) and City Pass (https://www.citypass.com). Both options offer discounted entry or multi-event passes in various cities and countries around the world. The multi-event pass is great because if you really want to hit the most popular spots in the city, they are all bundled together which gives you greater options.

Didn't the transportation expense add up?

One of the reasons why it is good to choose a large city for solo travel (for starters) is that the best way to get around the tourist areas is by foot or public transportation (train or bus). I don't ever recall ordering a taxi while in NYC. However, LA is a different story. You definitely need a car to get around. When I went to Washington D.C. for the first time, I rented car service, what I didn't know is that it was black car service, not Uber. I actually thought I had contacted a taxi but it wasn't. When I tell you that I thought that I belonged on the U.S. Executive Department, I wore it well. That was the absolute best service ever! The driver was amazing. He asked me if I was from there and I told him that it was my first time to the state. He was so excited to point out areas to go and where different sites were. One thing that stood out about my driver was a thoughtful gesture he did. I thought he was pulling into a gas station because he needed gas, at first, I thought that was awkward but the he asked me if I was hungry and I was a little hesitant to say yes but he went into the store and bought me some chips and a Coke as a welcoming gift. I tipped him well for his kindness. Maybe it was great customer service to some but he did it well.

Okay, I went off the topic, but I've always been able to keep my transportation expenses down using public transportation or stay in a location that I can walk the majority of the way. If I have to rent a car then I shop around. There are several websites that offer great deals and if you find coupon codes, then you might find substantial savings.

I frequently use a site called www.rentalcarmomma.com where I can find various coupon codes. Since I am a Budget Fastbreak member, I use her coupon codes every time. The best thing about Budget (www.budget.com) is that you can use their Pay Now or Pay Later option. I usually select the Pay Now option to get additional savings. You can also use a technique by making a reservation and shopping around a little more to see if that is the best deal. I usually just stick with Budget. Plus, I can practically zoom through the pickup/drop off process.

To be honest, sometimes you can just hit a good deal just by going directly through a car rental site. I've been able to get convertible sports cars for the price of an economy over the weekend just by a random chance.

Another great site to use is www.rentalcars.com. It's basically a search aggregator specifically for car rentals. It returns the best rates from the available rental car companies.

Solo Travel 101

How can I afford to travel solo, isn't it more expensive?

[ ] Set a travel budget

Let's do a little exercise and take the time out to fill in the following blanks. Hopefully, this will get you moving in the right direction.

MINI TRAVEL BUDGET

Write the Vision and Make it Plain - Habakkuk 2:2

Destination: **Estimated Budget:**

Maximum Amount that you can afford to spend.

	Est Amt	Actual Amount	Difference	Complete √
Flight				
Lodging				
Car Rental/Uber/Transportation				
Food				
Entertainment/Misc				
Total Amount				

The goal is to get you to putting your plan on paper

[ ]Ways to save

One of my favorite tools to save money without having to put a lot of effort into it is using an app called Digit (https://digit.co/). Digit analyzes your spending in order to estimate an amount to save for you automatically on a daily basis. The best part is that you can pause the savings for a specified amount of time, for however long that you choose, and restart when you need to. This is also a great option for you to use for an emergency fund or anything that you choose to do. It is linked to your checking account and the only minor drawback is if you need to withdrawal your money, it may take a day or two for the money to be deposited back into your account.

You can also select the amount to withdraw without having to totally deplete your savings. I've used it for a little over a year and it has not only contributed to savings but also any unexpected expenses that have popped up. You know how life can be sometimes! I hope that you check it out. ** One thing that I would recommend is that you keep a close eye on your budget because it will pull a percentage based on what the balance of your account. **

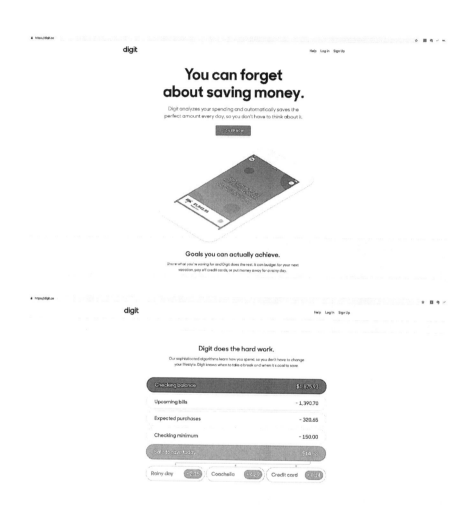

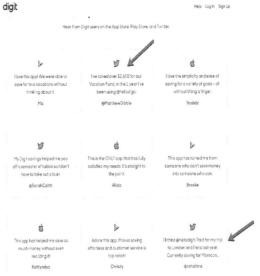

Have a travel fund account

I've shared some ideas with you on how to save for your trip, but I also think it is necessary to separate your savings to an account specifically for travel. You can either do this by opening a new account with your current bank or credit union or a completely different one and get a debit card associated with the account. You can use the card for travel purchases only, but do not put it in your wallet until you are ready to pack. This way, it helps you to not touch your funds and to keep your budget on point.

How to get the guts to travel solo

Don't overthink the process and what might happen. It's so easy to get caught up with all the qualms of solo travel, most are preconceived notions and the only way to overcome the fear is to actually do it. I guarantee that if you message most of the people in the travel forums of their thoughts on solo travel, they will tell you that it is the best thing that they've ever done for themselves. Quit thinking that it's going to be boring and change your mindset to focus on the places that you will see that you've never seen before, experiencing various cultures, and enjoying your life in that moment. Yes, there are times where it would be great for someone to be with you to experience some of the most amazing moments, you will soon get over. Just keep in mind to take in the moment.

HERE'S AN ASSIGNMENT FOR THOSE THAT NEED A LITTLE HELP MOVING FORWARD WITH THE SOLO TRAVEL PROCESS.

Your First Steps to Solo Travel
Start with one city/state at a time.

1. **Grab a map or go to Google Maps** and select some nearby states or a desired tourist location like NYC, Los Angeles, Chicago, or Miami

2. **Start researching things to do** in the city that you want to visit and start to make a list (*You can use the solo trip planner that I created for you in this book as a starter - write it down*) Let's say that you live in St. Louis and you would like to go to Chicago. Pull up Google Maps and type in St. Louis to Chicago and Google Maps will return the driving time. In this instance, about 4 hours, which is not bad for starters.

The best thing about Google Maps is that it will also return other methods of travel such as bus or air and give you details making planning your trip easy.

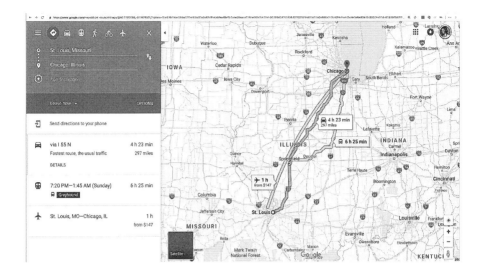

3.   Next, type in things to do in Chicago. It will return an array of suggestions to help spark your travel brilliance.

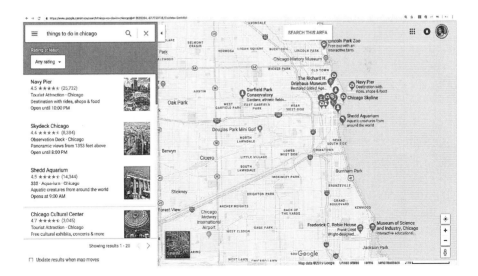

4.   ***Get connected*** with other travelers by using the various Facebook groups or any other online groups. This

helps you to be prepared. Once you start gathering information on the suggested places to stay or things to do, then do a little more research about them. Go to www.tripadvisor.com or even www.yelp.com and start to look these places up. There you can read the various reviews and check ratings in order to gauge your decisions.

For finding active Facebook travel groups, type the word "travel" in the search bar and select **Groups.** The search will return a listing of available travel groups you can join. There are general ones while others are by interests or other commonalities. Nonetheless, select one that appeals to you and search around, ask questions, and be engaged.

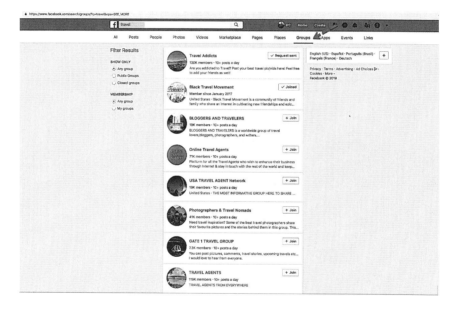

5.   *Set a date*. Choose one weekend, take a vacation day (Friday preferably).

6.   *Find somewhere to stay*. For starters, I won't through you into the whole house sharing idea, but so that you feel comfortable, start with a hotel. Still keeping the example above for a trip to Chicago, I decided to find you a hotel around the 4th of July weekend. I searched

hotels.com and came across a special for $37 per night, it was originally $114 per night. This option is considered specialty lodging so it wasn't a traditional hotel chain, it's more like a hostel. To take it a step further and verify the reviews, I headed over to tripadvisor.com and entered the hotel name to see the user ratings. It was a 4 out of 5 review out of 609 reviewers, which is extremely well. In this case, this would be a great choice, that is if you are not looking for luxury but something safe, clean, and a great location. This is just an example, but if you're looking for good deals from traditional hotel chains definitely search hotels.com or hoteltonight.com.

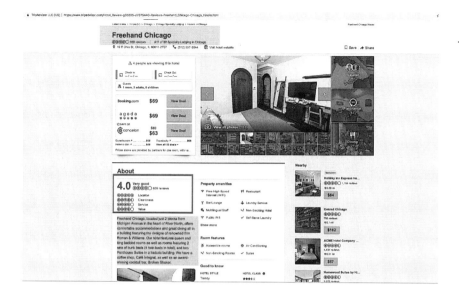

7.　　Once you made the move, head to my Facebook page (https://www.facebook.com/brilliantwanderer/) and post a pic of your first journey, I might just drop a little something in the mail to ya!

Congratulations!　You did it.　It's just that simple.

Safety for Solo Travelers

Travel Safety Tip!

** ONE WORD OF CAUTION **
WHEN USING PUBLIC TRAVEL GROUPS , DON'T GIVE ALL YOUR DETAILS ABOUT WHEN YOU ARE PLANNING TO TRAVEL, BUT AT LEAST REACH OUT AND ASK QUESTIONS FOR SUGGESTIONS ON WHAT TO DO, WHERE TO GO, OR ANY OTHER THOUGHTS YOU MAY HAVE ABOUT YOUR TRIP.

DO NOT REVEAL TOO MUCH PRIVATE INFORMATION REGARDLESS OF WHAT OTHER PEOPLE ARE SHARING. REMEMBER, THIS IS PUBLIC AND ANYONE COULD BE A PART OF THESE GROUPS, SO PLEASE USE YOUR BEST JUDGMENT ON SHARING PERSONAL DETAILS. **

Wandersafe App

Wander Safe is the app that empowers users to navigate their surroundings better and safer. With interactive and dynamic location-based maps and the help of **JENI**, your personal safety concierge who provides relevant safety advice and alerts the user upon you if you are entering an area that could be unsafe.

Arrive safe, and stay that way. See what is happening with reports of crime or unsafe areas from **JENI** through trusted data sources such as law enforcement so walk, run and enjoy the outdoors with greater confidence.

Location Sharing

Turn location tracking on for specific family or friends, in case of an emergency. On an iPhone it's known as Family Sharing/Find My Friends. My friend Tonda turned me on to this tip a few years ago. I was on the road traveling and it was a long turnaround trip but I was determined to be at this particular place supporting my friend and her family. On my way back home, I told her that I was going to drive straight through because I needed to get back as soon as I could. It was about a 6 hour drive ahead of me and I had already been on the road six hours early that morning. We both have iPhones so she told me to enable location tracking so that she

179

could check in from time to time to see where I was at. I thought to myself that is such a great idea and that's why I am sharing it with you. Safety first.

How to enable Share My Location:

1.   From your iPhone home screen, select the **Settings** button
2.   Select **Privacy**
3.   Select **Location Services**
4.   Select **Share My Location**
5.   Select the person that you want to share your location with

To stop sharing your location, turn off Share My Location. This hides your location from all of your family members and your

approved friends. And when you're ready to share your location again, you can turn it back on at any time. More info can be found on the Apple support page:
https://support.apple.com/en-us/HT201087

Google Maps also has a Location Sharing feature which is more universal and not device specific. The caveat to using Google Maps in general is that anyone can access it from anywhere and even if you lost your phone, you can connect via email to retrieve your information. No stress, no strain.

Solo Travel Safety Tip #2:

181

As mentioned earlier, my first solo trip far far away was to NYC back in the early 2000's. I spent a lot of time doing research about this city because everything that I heard about it made me extremely cautious. I've lived in some major cities, but this one was that granddaddy of them all. I was especially concerned about the subways and trains, partly due to the movies that I used to watch. Since I didn't know a soul in the city, I made sure that I was prepared. There were sites that had live videos of the city and people and I would study the culture, what people wore and how they looked in general. I don't know why I was so nervous, you would had thought I was going to another country where no one spoke English.

When I got there, I was in total awe of course, it's New York City but I tried to play it cool. I told myself that I would take pictures on the sly because I refused to walk around with a DSLR or stand in the middle of the walkways looking up at the tall buildings. I walked in rhythm with those around me straight face and all. My inner child was jumping for joy while my outward expressions were so very serious. I laugh at it now. I refused to do a lot of touristy things, though I did get around to doing some. People would ask me where I was from and I'd say Brooklyn, it worked for the most part. I remember jumping on a bus from Coney Island back to Brooklyn and I was the only person on the bus at the time so the bus driver and all were chatting along. He was about the only person I told that I wasn't from there and he, being a New

York native, said that I actually fit in pretty good except for my accent. I told him that I would work on that next time, we both laughed.

Now you don't have to be as overly cautious but as mentioned in the earlier post, please use your gut instincts.

The power of Social Media

If for whatever reason you don't have family or friends to share your trip details with and are in an extreme emergency, consider your Facebook travel group. The reason that I recommend me this, even though it's good to not share personal details online, there have been extreme cases where I've witnessed people reaching out for help in the Facebook groups and many, many concerned members come to the aid, by providing resources, praying, staying in touch with people, as well as contacting authorities, etc. on the persons behalf. I remember reading and following a post about some ladies being stranded in Puerto Rico or Dominican Republic (I believe) during a recent hurricane. It was pretty bad. One of the friends had an early flight back home before the storm had hit while her friends stayed and couldn't get home. Another post that I recall was someone in another country and their Airbnb host had kicked them out and threw their stuff out. The young lady felt very violated and threatened and scared. I remember being scare for her because the whole ordeal seemed very fishy. She was there by herself, but people were reaching out to her, some even offering to pay for her hotel room until she could catch a flight home. I think most people monitored the post until she updated her status of being back home and safe. It meant a lot to see this, but it definitely helped me to reconsider just how powerful and such influence that Social Media has. I have even seen similar posts and efforts on Twitter. People are definitely watching and very much in tune. So as a last resort, know that Social Media can be a life saver.

Location is everything

Where you stay on your solo trip is extremely important and the location is something that you need to take into consideration while planning out your trip. You definitely want to research the area thoroughly and make sure that it's not somewhere far off from the main areas, local transportation, and the airport. For first time or less experienced solo travelers, it's a good idea to stay in more populated areas.

Make copies of your ID

Just to be on the safe side and in case of an emergency, have on hand and provide a family member or trusted friend a copy of your ID and medical card information. Make sure that you and someone you know has a copy of your itinerary, including hotel and airline booking information. In fact, I user TripIt (www.tripit.com) to store and share my travel information. If you have a gmail account, then you will also have access to Google Drive. You can upload your documents here, share with only the people you want to have access to the documents and it's universal and can be accessed anywhere or anytime by smartphone, PC, iPad or tablet, etc.

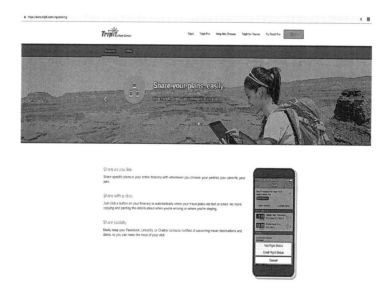

I lost my phone during my trip what do I do?

Phone Tip

Backup your phone before you leave for your trip.

Save your contacts to a Google Drive or Spreadsheet for easy access in case your phone is lost or stolen.

If by any chance you happen to lose or misplace your mobile phone, here's some things to consider. As a rule of thumb, enable your phone's tracking service before your travels. The next thing before you leave home is to back your phone up. These are precautionary measures, but can definitely save you a ton of unnecessary frustrations.

Do you have a second phone (old one that works)? Put it in your bag, you never know when you will have to re-enable it. You can also think about getting a pre-paid phone, if necessary.

Here are some suggestions in locating your phone:

1.   Don't panic. Try calling or sending a text to your phone.
2.   Use the "Find My Phone" feature by connecting to your mobile phone service provider via the internet
3.   Report the lost or stolen phone to your carrier. They will possibly give you the option to disable or swipe the phone clean. You might have to use your phone insurance at this point to get a replacement phone.

10 of my favorite and practical travel tools and tips:

1.   Ziplock bags (Large and Small) - Especially great when just using a carryon and you need to easily get through airport security. Place any toiletries in one bag and any items like laptop or electronic device cords in one large bag.

2.   Packing Organizer Bags - Makes packing your suitcase simple and organized.

3.   Secret compartment belt - A secret compartment belt (is like a fanny pack but flat) that you can wear in under your clothes when you travel. Just a good rule of thumb (separate your monies in various places in case you run into an unexpected loss of luggage, theft, or any other event that might cause you to lose your money or identity)

4.   Infinity/convertible dresses and jumpsuits - I absolutely love these. Convertible dresses/jumpsuits allow you to pack light and keep it simple. You can have several of these to switch out (wash) and while changing the style.

5.   Waterproof phone pouch - Best used at the beach, swimming pools, or water excursions.

6.   Extension cord or surge protector with USB ports - Don't leave home without it.

7.   Mobile apps - Whatever you need...There's an app for that!

8.   Tech Accessories holder - If you like to carry your mobile phone, a laptop or tablet, camera or any other tech tool, then you need the cords and cables with them. This allows you to keep them organized and in one place.

9.   Portable USB charger - I have about 4 of these. I take about 2 or 3. They are very small but these can be life savers to keep your electronics charged, especially for your mobile phone.

10.   A notepad and pen - You can never go wrong with this. Write down at least 3 important phone numbers (family or friends), address to where you are staying, and any other information that you might need just in case you lose your phone or belongings. You've got some points of contact.

11.   **Bonus** Smart Watch - In the case that you accidentally misplace or lose your phone, your smartwatch can come in handy. You will still have access to your contacts, text/email messages, GPS, and travel information...plus the ability to make calls. It just might be worth the investment.

Multi-State solo road trip

When starting out on a solo trip, if you don't mind driving, this can be fun. At least to clear your mind. I decided to do this some years ago during a holiday weekend. I wanted to go visit "Sweetie Pies" restaurant in St. Louis, Missouri and I actually mapped out some other things that I could do on the journey. I actually made a round trip leaving from one side of my state entering in to another side of my state, but in that trip (3 days - 1200 miles) I was able to visit 3 states and 4 cities within. On my way to St. Louis, took a quick detour to visit the World's Largest Gift Shop and Candy Store. Then I stopped off the beaten path and took in a mini tour of George Washington Carver's National Memorial in Diamond, Missouri. That was the most insightful experience ever. Then from there I made it to St. Louis, headed to Sweetie Pies and ate a scrumptious meal. While in St. Louis, I actually stayed on the campus of Washington University in their hotel and it was a great experience on their beautiful campus.

After leaving St. Louis, I charted my trip to Memphis, Tennessee to see the site where Dr. Martin Luther King was assassinated, visited Bourbon Street and headed to Little Rock, Arkansas to get a little closer to home. I stayed in Little Rock for the night and got up early the next morning to head to visit my family in Fort Smith. My aunt made me eat and rest for a bit before getting back on the road to make it back to my home town.

How I did this was just looking at the closest cities/states around and estimated a 2 to 3-hour drive per state (which isn't too bad) and just went for it. No regrets.

Tours: Contiki Tours

Contiki Tours is a fun way to travel with a group, whether you are solo or traveling with friends, if you're between the ages of 18 and 35. I first learned of Contiki watching MTV's The Real World, years ago. In fact, it was a sponsor for the show and often managed the various trips the cast members would make. Contiki offers affordable tours all around the world.

They offer guided and self-guided tours, but hotels/alternative lodging, most meals, and transportation is provided to each location depending on the package you select. You can choose to travel to several countries in Europe and have peace of mind that you will not be alone. Definitely good for solo travelers and/or a friend or two who is new to the travel journey.

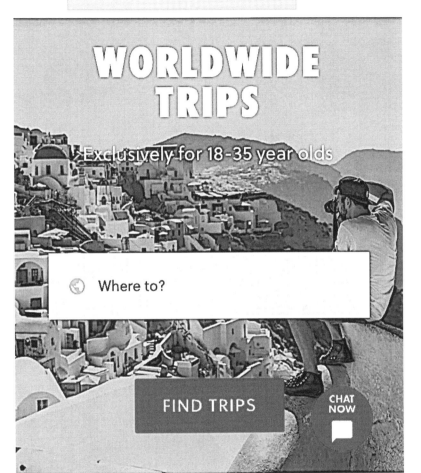

🔒 contiki.com　　🔄

☰　🔍 Search Contiki　　📞▾ 👤▾

FOOD EXPERIENCE

LEARN THE AUTHENTIC
ART OF THAI COOKING,
CHIANG MAI
Find out more

LAST MINUTE DEALS

50+ TRIP DEALS
Save up to 25% off trips
departing soon

REAL TRAVEL STARTS HERE

**DISCOVER OUR
EXPERIENCES**
How to turn a fun trip
into something life-

SAVE UP TO

$270

CHAT
NOW
💬

EUROPE
Greek Island ••• g
13 days trip, from ~~$2,420~~
~~$2,420~~

< 　 > 　 📤 　 📖 　 🗇

☰   🔍 Search Contiki   📞 ▾   👤 ▾

HOW IT WORKS

Details sorted

Accommodation, transport and a bunch of meals all sorted for you and included in the price of your trip.

CHAT NOW 💬

REAL. UNIQUE. LOCAL.

Discover a new way to travel Contiki & save 15%* on select trips worldwide.

‹   ›   ⬆️   📖   🗗

🔒 contiki.com   ↻

≡   🔍 Search Contiki   📞▾ 👤▾

HOW IT WORKS

18-35s only

〈 Experience it all with a crew of other young travellers from all around the world. 〉

REAL. UNIQUE. LOCAL.

Discover a new way to travel Contiki & save 15%* on select trips worldwide.

 CHAT NOW

〈   〉   ⬆️   📖   🗐

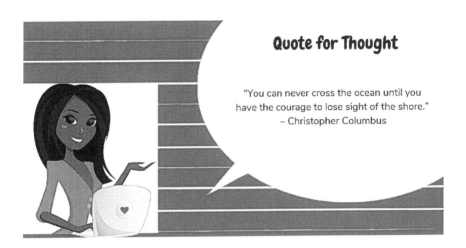

Quote for Thought

"You can never cross the ocean until you
have the courage to lose sight of the shore."
-- Christopher Columbus

Girls Trips, Guys Trips, and Group Trips

This segment is for group trips of any kind, whether it is a girls/guy trips, church group trips, groups that travel to a destination wedding or family reunion, there is something for everybody. If you check out the section under the guys trip, I broke down how much it would cost 8 men could go to the Super Bowl. These strategies can be applied to your trip planning for your group. I have also given various ideas to consider doing as a group. Let your imagination flow and be inspired!

Travel Quote

"Travel is more than the seeing of sights; it is a change that goes on, deep and permanent, in the ideas of living."
– Miriam Beard

Girls Trip Ideas

Let's be honest the saying holds true, Girls Just Want to Have Fun (okay, the guys do too) regardless of age. What better way to celebrate with your closest friends than to vacation together? Besides, this would be a perfect the time to just relax, unwind, and reconnect and not have to concentrate on the responsibilities of life, well...if but for a moment.

I have put together some ideas for you and your besties to consider that aren't too farfetched and expensive.

Beach or Island Getaway - Sundresses and Swimsuits is all you need for this trip. You can't go wrong with a beach or island getaway. There are so many local beaches that you can choose from in California, Florida, South Carolina, or even Hawaii. You can also choose islands that are not too far from the US, such as Mexico, the Bahamas, or Jamaica and make a fabulous weekend trip. Pack your bags and go!

Spa Retreat - Get pampered and relax. Bring your favorite book, iPad, music and great conversation. Maybe have a loose itinerary and let your friends move around on their own time but meet up for dinner. Just keep it simple and enjoy yourselves.

Wine Tour - Take the wine train through Napa Valley. You and your group will be able to meet local vintners, enjoy winery tours, partake in wine tastings on board, and engage in celebrity winemaker dinners.

Napa Valley Wine Train

Get Glam Shopping Weekend - LA or NYC Fashion Districts are the perfect place to you shop 'til you drop but find some great deals while you are at it. After shopping, you and your girlfriends should glammed up by getting a makeover. You could find a local MUA (makeup artist) or go to a local beauty counter to have your makeup professionally done, then pick your hottest or super classy outfit and go out for a night on the town. You could rent a limo or get an Uber Black Car service and travel by SUV or a super fab car and be escorted around time. Why not?

Live it up!!

Isn't it time to get the fellas together and hang out for a chill weekend? I know that guys love to have fun too, so I thought about some general things men could do to take the load off from the day to day of hard work and the cares of this life to just focus on the company of good friends and to have a good time. Find a way to make it a yearly tradition. Set a date and do it! Life is precious and if you have some great men in your life who are like brothers to you, then take the time out and make the most of the moment.

NBA All Star Weekend - This idea actually came from one of my close friends whose husband, his son, and a few of buddies do every year.

© Copyright NBA

Super Bowl Weekend

This one I would suggest that you start early because everything is expensive (airline tickets, hotels, car rentals, game day tickets). Let's take Super Bowl LIII (2019) which will be held in Atlanta, GA and you and 7 of your boys want to get together and go. The Super Bowl tickets are very expensive so this may not be the most cost-effective trip, but you can cut costs in other areas by renting a house and a couple of SUVs and splitting the cost. Another option would be to go and hang out in the city where the event is being held and attend all the festivities in the area then go to a nice sports bar for a watch party. If you are considering flying, the rates Again, start early -- as soon as the location for the next year is announced.

** Sample Breakdown of costs for the Super Bowl trip for eight men from Houston, Texas **

Total Cost for Super Bowl trip: $13,728 [$2,231.59 pp]
(including airfare, home rental, and car rental)

Optional Trip Cost (excluding airfare):

SUV Rental (x2) = Chevy SUVs $429.95 x 2 =$859.90 ($107.49 pp)
Gas SUV = $306 ($102 one way; $204 RT and let's say an additional $102 in the city) x 2 vans = $612 ($76.50 pp)

House Rental: $2833 total ($354 pp)

** Total Costs (w/SUVs) = $3998.90 (499.86 pp) **

Another option:

12 Passenger Van: $223.75 ($27.96 pp)
Gas Van: $396 ($132 one way; $264 RT with an additional $132 in the city) = $49.50 pp

House Rental: $2833 total ($354 pp)
** Total Costs (w/Van) = $3452.75 ($431.59 pp) **

Airfare: ($1716 RT per person) If plane tickets are too high for everyone's budget then you might consider driving.

For airfare rates, I looked a Google Flights and selected a date range. A calendar will pop up and show the prices for each day but keep in mind they are subject to change. The goal would be to select a return date with the lowest price and that will end up being the rate that you would get. I will explain how to use Google Flights in a later chapter.

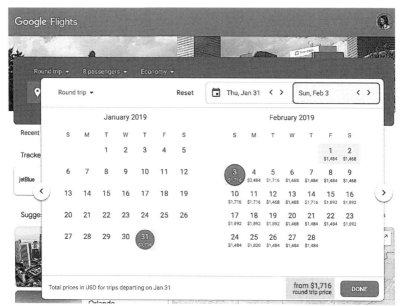

Optional: You can choose to drive from Houston, Texas to Atlanta, GA in a Chevy Suburban rental; I used www.tollguru.com to get an estimate of the gas cost for one way.

Gas Cost - Chevy Suburban: $306 ($102 one way; $204 RT and let's say an additional $102 in the city) x 2 vans = $612 ($76.50 pp)

Gas Cost - 12 passenger van: $396 ($132 one way; $264 RT with an additional $132 in the city) = $49.50 pp

Gas Cost for driving:

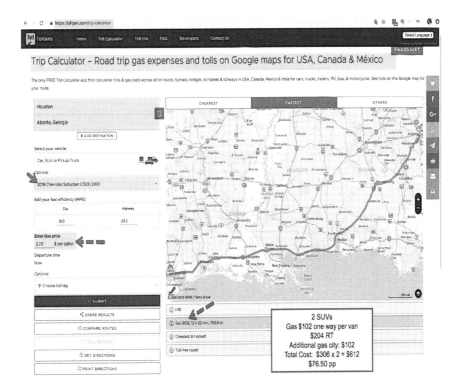

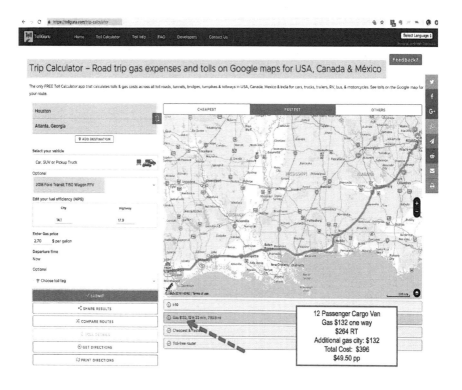

Car Rental Alternative: Chevy SUVs (x2) - $429.95 x 2 =$859.90 ($107.49 pp)

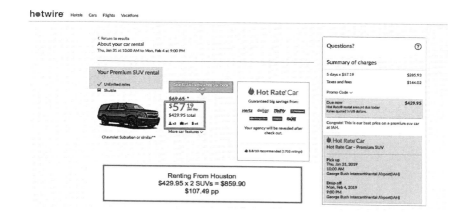

Car Rental Alternative: 12 passenger van - $223.75 ($27.96 pp)

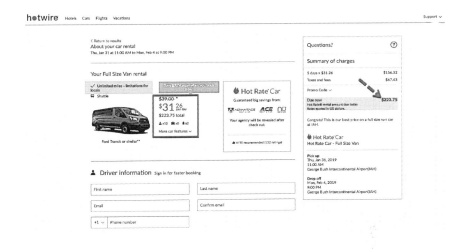

Home Rental: $2833 total ($354 pp)

When traveling with a large party, lodging can be quite costly especially hotels and with huge events such as the Super Bowl the options can be scarce and astronomically high. An alternative to this would be to rent out a home or condo. In the example below, I used www.vrbo.com (Vacation Rentals By Owner) website. This particular home has 6 bedrooms and sleeps 12 people, so you have more than enough space for the 8 of you to stretch out. You might consider grabbing some extra blankets and pillows for some of you (if not all) may need to make a pallet on the floor. I think that this is a great option because it might feel more like home to everybody or at least the good old days. You all can just stay up into the wee hours of the morning eating and talking noise to one another (in a good way). You know how you do it! My only advice is that when renting out someone else property, especially a home, please respect the property as if it was your own.

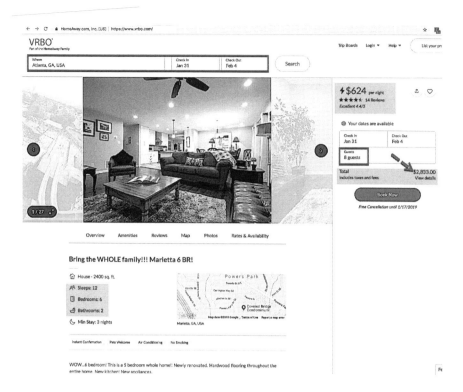

Car Rental: 2 Chevy SUVs $1761.70 ($220.21 pp) in Atlanta

This option is if you choose to fly into town and just rent a car. Because this time of the year is super busy, the rates are higher than normal. I chose 2 Premium SUVs so that there would be 4 men to each.

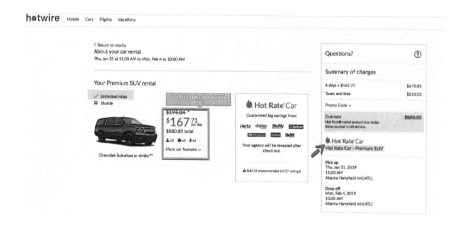

Car Rental (2 x 4Runner's in Atlanta): $1292.72 ($161.59 pp)

This was a secondary choice if you wanted to choose a Standard SUV. The savings would between the one above is about $400.

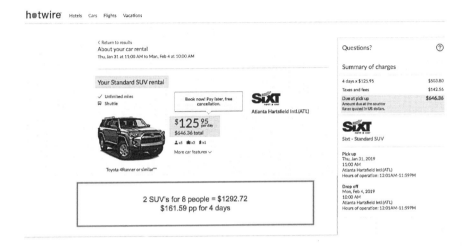

Golf Trip - If golfing is your thing, then call a few of your buddies up and head to Florida for a golf meetup. Florida has some of the most beautiful golf courses ever and the best scenery. Spend a couple of days on the course and try to schedule around the PGA Masters or Tour.

UFC Heavyweight Championship

Las Vegas baby!! A few years ago, I remember being in Vegas when there was a big Floyd Mayweather boxing match taking place. People were everywhere. There were fancy cars parading down the streets and you could just feel the energy in the atmosphere. This event draws thousands of people (especially men) into the city. Of course, you and your guys can't get bored because there is so much to do and you can eat for cheap. There are plenty of buffets!

Consider renting a two-bedroom timeshare unit (I recommend Wyndham) with adjoining rooms. You will have plenty of space to spread out and just kick back and chill. You can catch fairly good deals on flights to Las Vegas from most cities. I found the following through www.extraholidays.com. This site allows you to book vacation rentals whether you're a member or not. You can stay at some of the most popular vacation destinations throughout the United States, Canada, St. Thomas and Puerto Rico.The best part is that most of their units consist of suites with separate bedrooms, living/dining areas, partial or fully-equipped kitchens, washer/dryer as well as activities programs and extraordinary amenities.

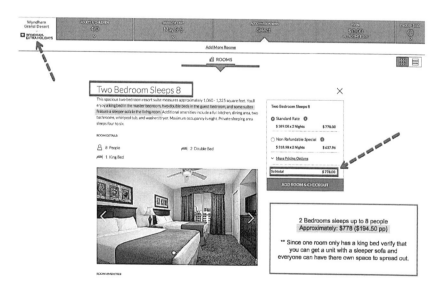

• ▪ Be prepared to get your airline tickets first! I cannot stress that enough as this is going to be your biggest expense and because they often fluctuate and sometimes not in your favor. Consider this: say that you are planning a year in advance then 1. Decide on the destination 2. Start everyone on a 3 - 6 month savings challenge to meet the goal 3. Once you have met your goals, then start your hunt for airfare especially if it is 6 months out, depending on the time of year you can catch some awesome deals. Purchase fares in off-season for a high season venture.

• Consider membership discounts for additional savings. You or someone in your group may have a membership such as AAA, Sam's Club, Costco, a credit union or even credit card rewards program that can be applied to some or part of the trip. You may also find discounts on tickets for attractions, dinners, and other events.

• Plan the number of days. My suggestion would be to start small like over a weekend (Fri - Sun/Thurs - Sun)

• Keep your invitee circle small as well as have an even number of people to balance out rooms and roommates.

• Planning a girl (or guys) trip can be a fun idea however it can be a stressful affair. It depends on what all the parties of your group like and what you can agree on as a whole.

• Know who you plan to travel with and what their travel style is like. Are they adventurous? Are they extremely laid back and cannot make decisions? Are they the type to sleep in all day and only care to stay close to the hotel? Are they tightwads or people that try to get over saying that they are broke, forgot their money or credit card? You should know the characteristics of the individual that your plan to travel with just by their actions and interactions with you on a friendship basis.

• Have a Plan B whether it is destination or change in itinerary.

• Create a community fund - You can establish your own travel fund which can be used for various activities. Save and plan the trip out a few months in advance. Set a portion aside to fund your savings account on a weekly or monthly basis according to the amount each of you all agree to pitch in. Later in this section of the book, I will introduce a couple of apps that you can use to pull the funds together.

• Use online tools to organize your plans and create a trip itinerary. A great site for the organizer to use is www.travefy.com. See more information later in this chapter.

• Create a private Facebook page for your travel group to share important updates, documents, itineraries, contact information, and any other pertinent information; use can also use Google Drive as a backup as well. However, the benefit to using a Facebook page is that you can interact and keep everyone informed and engaged. This keeps the enthusiasm up for everyone.

• Create WhatsApp Chat/Text Group Chat - perfect for communication especially if your group splits up while traveling and you need to connect quickly to share a change of plans, emergency info, etc. ** WhatsApp is an excellent group messaging app. They've recently added a new feature that allows only admins to send out messages in Groups, that way no one is bogged down with erroneous messages that can create confusion.

Trip planning, sharing itinerary, splitting bills, etc are all the components of organizing a trip but trying to figure out how to put it all together and communicate the information can be challenging. That's why I've composed a few of the best apps out there to use for group planning.

•   **WHEREFOR** (wherefor.com) allows you to enter a budget and see where you can go. I actually love this website because it is budget based. Just set a airfare and hotel budget for up to 8 travelers and it will return suggested cities and countries that you can travel to. This would be great to use when planning your group trip. Gather your members together and you all can decide where you want to go based on the agreed budget. The best part is that either one is optional, you don't have to purchase both as a packaged deal. You might just use the site to find a place to go and purchase the tickets at the best rate that they offer excluding the lodging arrangements.

See how far others have gone

209

- **TRAVEFY** (https://travefy.com/) is an all in one app best used for group travel planning, itinerary creation and sharing, as well as group expense management. It even includes a feature for group chat/discussions. This is basically all your group would need to keep everything in order and everyone on one accord.

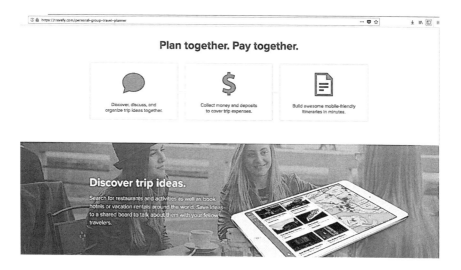

Make sure everyone's on the same page.
Stay organized with detailed, mobile-friendly itineraries.

• **PLANAPPLE** (www.planapple.com) This is a cool website to use to help you collect your travel information in one place. The group can discuss travel plans and keep in on going to refer to at any time. Travelers can access info from their smart phones or tablets, as well as get and share recommendations with one another.

• **SPLITTR** (www.splittr.io) - Splittr is an expense app that helps you to split group expenses on vacations, with your roommates or any other group activity. Simply add expenses as you go and Splittr will tell you who is next to pay and who owes whom how much.

They provide a great scenario on their app store preview page (https://itunes.apple.com/us/app/splittr-expense-splitting/) and I thought it would help explain the value of using this app for your planning purposes:

Use case: *So you are on a trip with 4 of your friends and you stop to get gas. It totals to $127. Instead of having to calculate and split yourself, you can just add the expense and let Splittr calculate the portions for you.*

It also helps you to keep tab on those in your group that do not pay right then and there but will do so. Splittr keeps everything managed and organized perfectly.

It's that simple!

iPhone Screenshots

- **TRIP ADVISOR** (www.tripadvisor.com) - This is my all-time go to app/website of them all and as you can tell, I've referred to it many times throughout this book. I use it for checking reviews on hotels, events/attractions or anything that would have a trend of people attending. You will find a variety of tips that you need to know and even can engage in community forums to query others' experiences. The mobile app is convenient as it acts as an on-hand guide, just in case you need last minute information. You can also track your trip information in case you forget your paperwork.

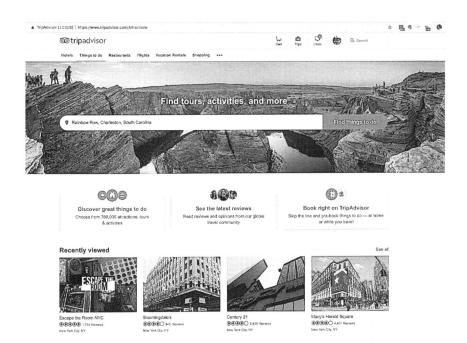

- **PRAVA** (http://pravaapp.com/) - Travel with friends and family is fun but clunky - you have to juggle different tools / apps before the trip, during the trip and after the trip. Need an easier way? Say hello to Prava. Keep all of your group's trip plans, details, photos, expenses and experiences in one simple place. This might by far be one of my favorite recommendations. Check it out for yourself.

See the following section for an excerpt of the functionality of the Prava app from their Google Play Store page: PRAVA

Prava is a free travel app that makes it easy for you to:

o   **PLAN THE TRIP** - Create your trip group, chat and build the travel itinerary (agenda).

o

o   **MAKE THE TRIP** - Capture and instantly share travel photos, expenses, locations and notes (blog) of the travel with your trip group.

o

o   **PUBLISH THE TRIP** - Publish the shared travel photos and travel notes (blog) together as a group to your contacts and other Prava users. Let them get inspired and connect with you. The trip itinerary, expenses, chat, locations and private photos remain private within the group. You can choose not to publish the trip as well ☐

o

o   **EXPLORE TRIPS** - Discover trips published by your contacts and other Prava users, connect with them, get inspired and plan your next travel.

Prava frees you from juggling multiple tools for group travel such as chat app, to-do app / notepad, expense app / bills, various social media for photos and blogs - and having to go back to them again for memories. Plus, Prava is the world's first group travel app which is also a social media for publishing and exploring trips.

Group Travel Tours

Travel Tours for Young Adults:

Contiki Tours: (www.contiki.com) - Where do I start? I learned of Contiki years ago watching a show called Real World. They would send their cast members off to a destination and it always looked so cool. They cater to young adults ranging from 18 - 35. I actually think that they have some of the best rates for international travel tours available. You can select tours from one week to over

4 weeks and can also filter to find one ranging in your group members budgets.

Check out the European Magic 10-day, 8 countries tour below:

Under 30 Experiences (www.under30experiences.com) is a company providing travel experiences for travelers between the ages of 21 and 35. Their goal is to show that travel can be fun, affordable, and hassle free so you don't have to worry about coming up with a plan.

Here is a sample trip that I put together using Under 30 Experiences and Google Flights. My traveler(s) would be going to Costa Rica from Dallas, Texas.

Trip Details:
Trip Length: 5 Days/4 Nights
Trip Package: $645
Airfare: $652 (using Google Flights)
Approximate Trip Cost: $1300

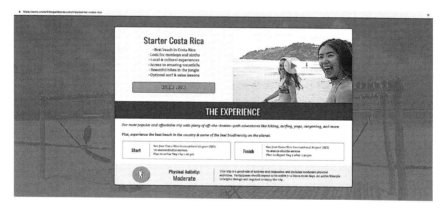

What's Included

We've got you covered:

-5 day / 4 nights in bungalows with roommates
-4 Breakfasts and 4 dinners
-Airport transportation to and from San Jose Costa Rica International Airport (SJO)
-El Cocal community cooking experience
-Under30Experiences Trip Leader
-The chance to meet some kick-ass people
-Taxes always included, never hidden fees, & NO blackout dates
-Book with confidence: it's free to switch your trip more than 30 days out

*Travelers responsible for international airfare to and from Costa Rica
*Accommodations can vary but will be the same quality
*Transportation to optional salsa & yoga not included

When should I book my flight?
Plan to arrive Day 1 by 1:00 pm and to depart Day 5 after 1:30 pm local time
*Please wait to book your flight until you receive an email from us with more details

DURATION:	EARLY SIGNUP: $645	REGULAR: $845
5 DAYS / 4 NIGHTS	Save $200 & taxes included!	Or only $195 down!

BOOK NOW **TRIP FAQ**

🛖 TRIP OVERVIEW | 📖 FULL ITINERARY | 🚵 TRIP DETAILS | 📅 VIEW CALENDAR

217

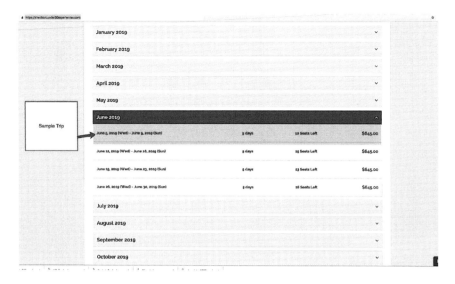

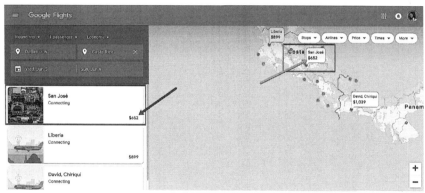

General Group Tours:

Cosmos (www.cosmos.com) - is a tour company that's been around for more than 50 years and offers affordable tour packages for groups of 8 or more persons. They offer an option known as Cosmo Lite that would be great for a group trip because the length is much shorter than a more in-depth exploration of countries. However, the short-term tours that they offer allow you to cover really great grounds. Most of which start at about $899 per person for about 7 days. Check out their website and order a brochure so that you and your group members can go through and determine where you want to go. Make it fun!

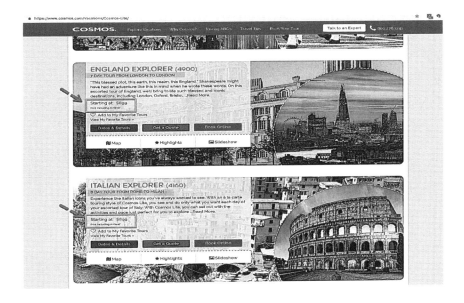

Affordable Tours: (www.affordabletours.com) is another travel company with great reviews. They aggregate various tours and provide you with the most affordable prices out there.

Intrepid Travel: (www.intrepidtravel.com) is a travel company specializing in small group tours and adventures in more than 120 countries. They offer travelers an opportunity to experience the culture by living like the locals through their guided tours.

I've seen tours as low as $489 so make sure you check out their travel deals.

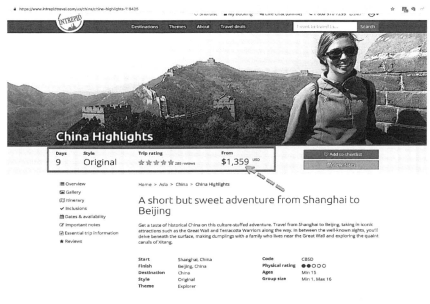

A short but sweet adventure from Shanghai to Beijing

Home > Asia > China > China Highlights

Get a taste of historical China on this culture-stuffed adventure. Travel from Shanghai to Beijing, taking in iconic attractions such as the Great Wall and Terracotta Warriors along the way. In between the well-known sights, you'll delve beneath the surface, making dumplings with a family who lives near the Great Wall and exploring the quaint canals of Xitang.

Start	Shanghai, China	Code	CBSD
Finish	Beijing, China	Physical rating	●●○○○
Destination	China	Ages	Min 15
Style	Original	Group size	Min 1, Max 16
Theme	Explorer		

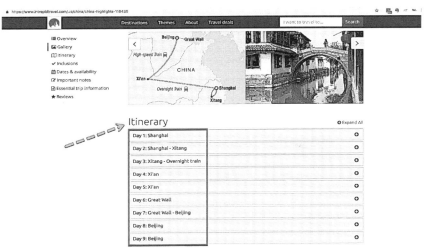

Itinerary

☉ Expand All

Day 1: Shanghai	⊕
Day 2: Shanghai - Xitang	⊕
Day 3: Xitang - Overnight train	⊕
Day 4: Xi'an	⊕
Day 5: Xi'an	⊕
Day 6: Great Wall	⊕
Day 7: Great Wall - Beijing	⊕
Day 8: Beijing	⊕
Day 9: Beijing	⊕

Discount Passes

Go City Passes for Groups

Go City Cards provide admission to multiple attractions for one low price. With this pass, you don't have to pay anything at the gate. What makes that also beneficial is that the more that you do the more you save. The Go City Cards are available for both domestic and international attractions. They offer both group discounts and student discounts. Check out their website at www.smartdestinations.com for more information on Group Travel cards as well as for Student Discounts.

Travel for Seniors

You've worked hard all your life and raised a family, now it's time to live. Many seniors live on a fixed income or are very budget conscious though they have saved well. I recently read an article about an 80-year-old plus lady that is retired who lives on a cruise ship.

There is a cruise company known as Story Lines (www.storylines.com) that offers affordable cruise condos you can you can live in full or part-time in order to see the world by sea. The cabin is not like a traditional cruise ship cabin, but more of like a studio with living space. It's an all-inclusive living arrangement that includes food, drinks, spas, a hair salon, plenty of activities and entertainment and much more. I'm not quite sure if that is your plan for retirement, but it could be an option. The bottom line is to live and enjoy your life to the fullest.

AAA: (www.aaa.com) is a household name that not only offers the common member excellent discounts on a full travel experience but also provides a network of resources for senior travel and touring. Be sure to download their smartphone app so that you will have all the information you need on hand.

AARP: (www.aarp.com) is a seniors' one stop shop for information they can offers amazing discounts for Seniors in general. Like AAA, they offer full travel benefits including airfare, hotel, car rentals and cruises.

Stride Travel: (www.stridetravel.com) is the place to find all types of travel tours for Seniors.

All Senior tours, river cruises, expedition cruises, and adventures. Find the best guided trips and expert planned vacation and holiday packages. Average rating of 4.6 for all Senior Travel trips.

Typically, most major airlines offer a special group booking option for a party of 10 or more travelers which may include special pricing. The best thing to do is to call the airline of your choice directly. They may offer you the best deal available. Should you choose to do some research yourself, then start with Google Flights or www.wherefor.com. Follow the scenario below of a trip with 8 travelers from Los Angeles. Check out the set budget and the actual trip cost!

1.   Set a budget for both hotel and roundtrip airfare for 8 people at $9600 ($1200 per person)

2.   The search then returns all the possible destinations within the travel budget.

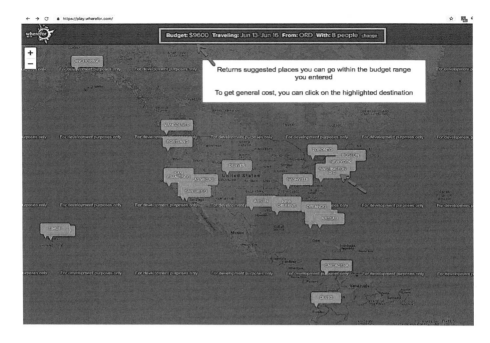

3.   In this example, the group decided to go to Washington D.C. Excellent choice! They are able to go for about $6000 less than their set budget. The total trip with roundtrip airfare would cost this group $3576.66 or $447.08 per person. Talk about savings!!

226

Group Cruises

I believe that one of the most affordable ways to travel with a group is to go on a cruise. After you figure out where you want to go and how you will get to the departure port, either by plane, train, or automobile, then all you have to do is board the ship and sail away! That's basically it.

A cruise is basically an all-inclusive deal: Room, all you can eat buffet, entertainment and dreamy destinations. The only thing that you would have to take into account are any extra expenses you would incur (gratuity, excursions, souvenirs etc.) but even those things can be included in your planning. Cruise lines have everything well thought out. They really want you to enjoy the journey without the stress of how you will be able to afford it. You can find deals for well in under $300 per person.

Benefits of Using a Travel Agent for Group Bookings

One of the main benefits of using a travel agent is that they can take the hassle out of planning and organizing your trip. They can wear the hat of coordinator and cater to the needs of your group. Travel Agents can handle the airline and hotel bookings, set the deadlines for deposits and take payments so that you don't have to worry about enforcing the rules or be taken advantage of. They can also help you strategize a plan of things to do while visiting as well as provide additional resources and deals for excursions and events. The major role that you will have to play after that is to be the group leader during your trip. Breathe.

I have included some of the best travel agents that I know of in the resource section of this book that can handle the job and do it exceptionally well.

Getting around your destination as a group

This sounds so simple but could definitely be an expense that could add up if not planned properly. Depending on the size of your group, you may not want to split up too much especially if you are in an unknown territory for the majority of travelers. Renting and keeping up with several cars could be pretty chaotic so to make things more organized and cost effective then consider renting a passenger van or booking Ubers.

Rent a passenger van for parties of 6 or more

In my earlier example of a trip to the Super Bowl, I found a deal to rent a 12-passenger van for as low as $27.96 per person for the entire trip. All you have to keep up with is one vehicle and of course all members of your group.

Car Rental Alternative: 12 passenger van - $223.75 ($27.96 pp)

UberXL

The second option would be to rent and UberXL (www.uber.com). It all depends your actual destination, how much traveling will getting around entail and how far you would need to go per day. Depending on the group, you could probably pool together funds for transportation only, which could include Uber or public transportation, thus excluding having to rent a car. Better to count up the cost before you use this option.

Business Travelers

This book is for entrepreneurs, startup founders, remote and location independent professionals, road warriors, digital nomads, and small business owners who are budget conscious but travel for the purpose of conducting business related activities. You could be at the beginning of your entrepreneurial journey or have been operating independently (of Corporate America) for many years. Either way, travel expenses can be out of control if not carefully planned and properly budgeted. Even though most are tax deductible, you still have to pay out of your own pocket and it might not seem so justifiable. In fact, it may give you the impression that taking that trip might not be a great option after all.

My goal is to share at least one resource or tip that can help you cut down on your travel expenses as well as to provide you with ideas to make the most out of your travels. Hopefully the information in this book will help reduce the time and frustration of scouring the internet to find information that is valuable to you and your business. The other caveat is you could use some of these ideas to create an additional revenue stream for your business. It's all in how you look at it. Are you ready? Wheels up!

"Instead of thinking outside of the box, get rid of the box."
- Anonymous

"A mind that is stretched by a new experience
can never go back to its old dimensions."
– Oliver Wendell Holme

Acquiring great deals as a Business Traveler

A friend of mind, Brenda Small, who is a Real Estate Broker and a Business Leader, shared some tips with me for budget conscious business travelers who are seeking the best deals and preferential treatment at hotels:

- Call ahead to hotels to get information specifics about the hotel, preferred location and amenities to gauge the quality of customer service
- Make connections with the hotel staff; Upon arrival, you will have a name to reference and get desirable treatment during the stay
- Ask for deals or special rates
- Consider booking at independent chains and boutique hotels because:
- They provide a greater guest experience over the traditional chain standard of service
- A boutique hotel is smaller than an average hotel, having between 10 and 100 rooms, which allows the staff to offer more of a personalized service
- They provide better business amenities, services, and resources; a local one that I'm familiar with offers black car service around the metropolitan area
- They are upscale chic and are economical

• Have a pleasant attitude. Smile and make small talk. Give genuine compliments to the service staff. This will leave a positive impression with the staff and they will go out of their way to make sure you have the best guest experience.

One thing to note. Many of the large hotel chains, such as Marriott, actually own boutique hotels also known as The Autograph Collection. Sounds ritzy huh? The best part about this is you can use your rewards toward your stay and reap the benefits of your membership.

Hotel Stays and Hotel Alternatives

When traveling for business, I believe the culture and environment in which you stay is important. It should be a place that nurtures your inspiration, creativity and be free from unnecessary distractions.

Reducing your travel expenses for lodging doesn't mean that you have to reduce the quality. There are plenty of hotels out there competing for your business so the goal for you would be to determine which one you would reap the most benefits from. You might have already established membership to a hotel loyalty program, which may be adding points to your frequent flyer miles, but I wanted to share with you some hotel alternatives that might be comparable and save you money.

Co-Working and Co-Living Spaces - For the Digital Nomads/Location Independents (working on the road):

Millennial startup founders are changing the common workplace as well as eliminating the need to rent out conventional office space. Communal (shared) working and living arrangements, better known as co-working and co-living spaces, have become a phenomenon and very appealing to this population plus it's a great opportunity to connect with other founders. It's a social experience.

One way I would describe this, in order to give you a mental picture, is to think of a public library with open areas to study as well as private study coves. It's an environment that influences highly productive and focused individuals to get their creative juices flowing.

Co-Working and Co-Living Spaces are not limited to just startup founders but remote workers or anyone who is location independent and needs a space to work at while on the road. This concept is also great if you have a small team and need to provide housing.

Maybe you need a sabbatical to help you to regroup, this way you will have an on-demand workspace to stay focused while only being just a few steps away from your sleeping quarters after burning the midnight oil. This type of setup encourages greater collaboration while fostering innovation. Most of the co-working spaces are membership driven but many of them offer day passes on an as-needed basis.

Before you jump on the Co-Living bandwagon, consider it living in a college dorm with complete strangers. You may have your own private room or you may share the space with others. It's co-habitation.

Here are a few resources to check out:

www.regus.com - *Regus* has been around for a long time and has provided its visitors with office space, co-work space, meeting rooms, a business lounge, virtual offices and memberships that will give you access to any location *Regus* resides.

www.wework.com - *We Work* is a widely known company that offers coworking spaces for the startup and entrepreneurial communities.

www.techspace.com - Designed specifically for scale-up teams, *Techspace* coworking spaces offer a plug-and-play membership to accelerate business growth.

www.venturex.com - Their vision is to provide a *Venture X* in every major city globally where members can connect, be inspired, improve their business/careers and experience fulfilling rich lives. They have multiple locations across the United States and are currently expanding into the international markets.

www.spaceswork.com - *Spaces* is a full service, creative working environment with a unique entrepreneurial spirit, where ideas develop, businesses build and relationships evolve; What really makes *Spaces* unique is the community they cultivate, they have an international network of mobile workspaces, and host business events, speakers and networking lunches.

www.roam.com - *Roam* is a network of global co-living spaces that provide everything you need to feel at home and be productive the moment you arrive. Their values are Comfort, Community and Productivity.

www.venturefounders.com - *Venture Founders* is not only a website that offers a plethora of valuable information for founders, they've also included an extensive list of co-working/co-living spaces.
https://venturefounders.com/coworking-directory-usa/

cowoli.com - CoWoli is Co-Working meets Co-Living

www.podshare.co - PodShare builds affordable shared housing across Los Angeles

sun-and-co.com - Sun and Co. is the first co-living and co-working community in the whole Mediterranean Coast. A place for freelancers, entrepreneurs, location independent workers, digital nomads and anyone looking for a great work and leisure balance.

Corporate Housing

Corporate Housing is known in the corporate world as temporary housing for employees, often those being relocated to another state and is included in their compensation package. Typically, corporate housing are fully furnished apartments that have everything that you could possibly need to and to make your transition into a new city as smooth as possible.

www.corporatehousing.com
www.2ndaddress.com

Homes2 Suites by Hilton (home2suites3.hilton.com)

Home2 Suites, is an all-suite, extended stay property. I had to include them because it is one of my absolute favorite places to stay when I'm on the road. I love the vibe of the hotel and the generously spacious and well-furnished rooms that they offer. Honestly, the first time that I had learned of them was during a bad ice storm in my city and our neighborhood was without power for quite some time. It was miserably cold and I had company in for a visit. Because it was almost a dire emergency and our options were scarce, the staff had offered us a great deal and we were able to stay in the largest suites because there was four of us. When I tell you that we could have all done summersaults in the room without worrying about bumping into one another, it was simply amazing. Not only did we have two queen size beds, we also had a sleeper sofa. Enough for everyone to spread out. For business purposes, you have plenty of workspace whether in your room, communal areas in the lobby or business center.

Wyndham Resort Suites (https://www.extraholidays.com)

Don't let the name fool you. You could be hosting a retreat, business boot camp, or conference in one of the locations

Wyndham Resorts cover. Not only could this be a great place for you to lodge but your attendees as well, especially if people would like to save more by doubling up in room occupancy. Like Homes2 Suites, Wyndham give you all the amenities that you or your guests would need for the course of a week or weekend, depending on the length of your event. They also so additional rates for special memberships like AAA, AARP, as well as a Senior Discount.

Rental Homes

Stay with me here, I don't want to lose you with this idea. This is for businesses or a startup with a team. Take for instance, you and 3 others of your team members are pitching your business at SWSX Pitch in Austin but want to arrive a few days before in order to get settled in and brush up on your pitch and stay a little longer to take part in the other activities. Because this is a very large and highly attended event, prices more than double almost triple because every place is in high demand. An option to think about would be to rent a home out for your team and split the cost. To be honest, with this type of event you would need to plan well in advance, about 6 months to a year out, to get the lowest rate. In that case, vrbo.com (Vacation Rentals by Owners) would be a great place to start and you would have the space you need with the luxury of having your team all in one space to eliminate coordination issues and schedules.

Business Ready Homes on AirBnB

AirBnB is the champion of the sharing economy for home and living space rentals which has parlayed into additional solutions such as providing rentals specifically for business travelers: https://www.airbnbforwork.com/.

Some of the benefits of this option for your company is that your company manage travel spending with streamlined reporting and dashboards. It also includes flexible cancellations and self-check-in for business trips. You may be also excited to know that it could also reduce your travel expenses by 40% compared to traditional hotel stays.

Stay Alfred (www.stayalfred.com) - What is Stay Alfred? It is the largest short term furnished rental firm that operates in major downtown neighborhoods across the nation. Even though they are in downtown areas where rates are a little higher, the access to the options are great for small group stays. Many of the guest state that it's a cross between a hotel and a home, so you get the best of both worlds. You can find their current deals which a link is listed at the bottom of the page on their website.

**Hotel... Vacation rental...
We're the best of both worlds.**

Located in the best downtown neighborhoods, Stay Alfred's upscale travel apartments offer the space and amenities of a vacation rental combined with the quality and consistency of a boutique hotel. For your next trip, let us be "Your place in the city."

Tax Deductions for Hotel Alternatives

I recently came across an article on the Nolo website entitled: *How to deduct lodging costs when you travel for business and stay at an Airbnb or similar rental.* It answered a simple question as to whether one could deduct the expenses of staying at places using websites like AirBnb, VRBO, or HomeAway? According to the article, it is actually true that you can claim a partial deduction of your stay. The writer precautions the readers that there are strict requirements by the IRS that you must meet. Here are a few tips that the article provides:

1.   You Must Have a Business
2.   Your Travel Must Be for Business

237

3.   You Can Deduct Lodging for One
4.   Only Lodging Expenses for Business Working Days
are Deductible

Read the article in its entirety at *www.nolo.com*.

Source: Deducting Business Travel Costs When You Rent via Airbnb by <u>*Stephen Fishman*</u>*, J.D.*

Office Space on Demand

Maybe you have a day trip to a city to meet with potential partners or other business engagements and you need a place to work or host a meeting. Starbucks may be too small and a restaurant may be too informal but there are affordable options to rent a workspace, desk, or office for the day or a few hours. As mentioned earlier, *Regus* (www.regus.com) has office space to rent whether you are in town for a day or you need one to operate out of in your home state, but there are more companies with similar services and variable price ranges. You have the option to rent offices, board rooms, conference or meeting rooms and still be able to stay within a reasonable budget.

https://www.sharedesk.net/

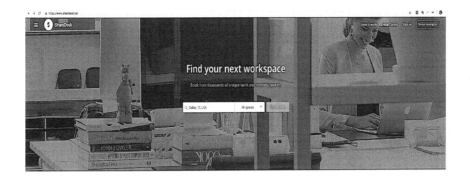

On-demand workspace, when you need it.

Book a coworking space, business center, or shared office space nearby.
Discover spaces to rent by the hour, day, or month.

This particular search for conference spaces in Dallas to rent out were as low as $54 per hour.

www.breather.com - Simple Description: *Breather,* A space to work, meet and focus.

Hourly Spaces (www.hourlyspaces.com) - *Hourly Spaces* allows business owners to both find a workspace but to also rent out your workspace or apartment while you are away.

LiquidSpace (www.liquidspace.com) - *LiquidSpace* is a search aggregator that will help individuals in finding co-working, business centers, sublets or landlord spec suites. In times past, any time of spaces were very limited or very expensive to rent out and holding fee hosted events at places like libraries were very limited. Now you can select a nice space to match your brand and quality of services that you provide.

Hotels and primarily any location that has "space" has caught on to the value of the on-demand economy and it has become a win-win situation for both the space providers and the businesses that need them.

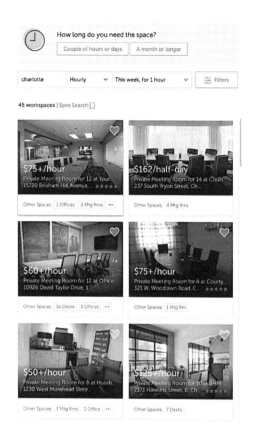

Frequent Traveler and Reward Membership Programs

Free night stays, free flights or upgraded seat class, discounted car rental are just some of the major perks of being apart of a loyalty rewards program. I'm certainly not a guru in this area, but I know that there are plenty of experts out there that have perfected the strategy to maximize your points. Here are a few bloggers that you can reference:

The Points Guy - thepointsguy.com
Frugal Travel Guy - www.frugaltravelguy.com
Nomadic Matt - www.nomadicmatt.com
FoundersCard

Like anything great, frequent travel miles and rewards must be built up in time...but maybe you are just starting out and you don't know how to get started but want to get in as quickly as possible, then check out **FoundersCard** (www.founderscard.com).

FoundersCard is an all in one membership specifically designed for entrepreneurs. *FoundersCard* has a wide spectrum of benefits for your business including travel reward programs with hotels and airlines, travel services such as ground transportation and a free 6-month membership with CLEAR, business service discounts, premium access to exclusive membership programs and additional benefits such as retail, health and lifestyle.
(https://founderscard.com/benefits)

Membership perks are subject to change at any time and there is an annual membership fee.

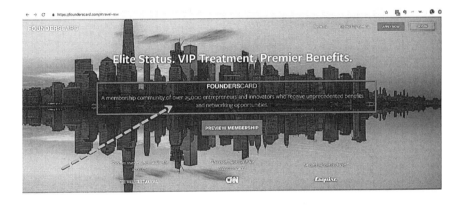

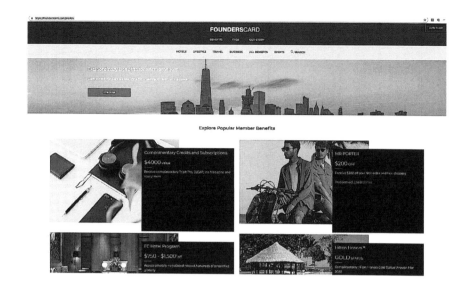

Saving on Airport Lounges

Several years ago, I remember traveling on a long trip and found myself stuck in a huge airport, I was hot and a bit overwhelmed with anxiety. I had stumbled upon an exclusive first-class lounge which I did not have membership to and had so wished that I did. I absolutely did not want to stay in a crowded boarding area just people watching plus I find it hard to concentrate or read with the level of stress that particular trip brought about. It was at that time that I started reading up on airport lounges and memberships that I had come across the *LoungeBuddy* app and realized that it was possible to have access without an actual membership. These can truly be a life saver in more ways than one. Before you pay for these services, check your credit card benefits as you may have free access to lounges in airports around the world.

LoungeBuddy (www.loungebuddy.com) - Stop now and go download this app on your phone. From basic to luxe, there is a lounge to fit your budget or taste. *LoungeBuddy* revolutionizes the airport experience by giving any traveler the ability to discover, book, and access premium airport lounges worldwide. With *LoungeBuddy*, all travelers can have instant access to any of the

244

lounges in their network excluding the need for memberships, elite statuses, or first-class tickets.

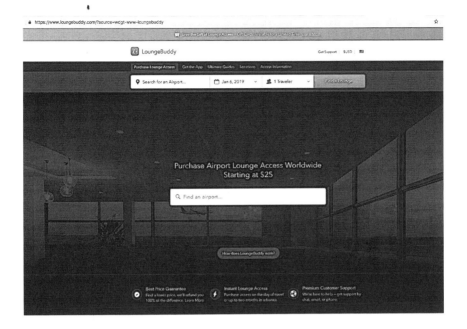

Minute Suites: (https://minutesuites.com) - *Minute Suites,* offers a private retreat that combines the positive effect of a power nap along with binaural beats to help travelers reduce stress and anxiety during their travel journey. If you have an extended layover and sitting in the terminal boarding area is just not your cup of tea, especially when you want to rest your eyes, then *Minute Suites,* might be a great option for you.

They have a shower facility fully stocked with a towel, body wash and additional toiletry needs. Their private suites have a daybed sofa with a sliding trundle bed for extra sleeping space, fresh pillows, and blankets, including a sound-masking system to omit outside noises from entering. Each room has a computer with a 32″ screen equipped with high-speed internet, flight tracking information, and cable television.

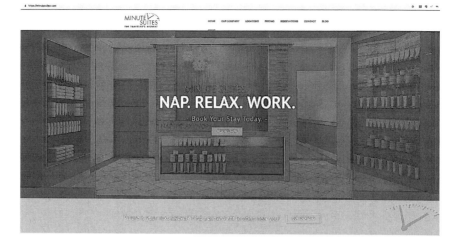

Small tip: *Airport Prayer Chapels are also great to retreat and find a little peace and quiet for a few minutes.*

Semi-Private Charter Jet

Caught your attention, didn't I? I know what you're thinking. How could I possibly include a resource like a private jet in a book that is supposed to help me save money? Well, guess what? There are actually services around that offer an affordable way to fly privately without busting your budget. While areas of operation are limited, who knows, you might be in the area and need to get to the destination within JetSuiteX flight route.

JetSuiteX - (www.jetsuitex.com) - is where you can enjoy the best of private travel at not-so-private fares. Avoid the traffic and airport madness when you fly exclusively between our private hangar and go from parking to take off in minutes. Check into your flight in just seconds and grab a complimentary beverage in our private lounge before seamlessly boarding your flight. No lines, no crowds, and no jetways. (Taken from their website)

Photo Credit: JetSuiteX

Once onboard, you can enjoy:
- Comfortable leather seats
- Business class legroom
- Power outlets at every seat
- Full flight attendant service
- Complimentary gourmet snacks, beer, wine and spirits
- No overhead storage bins for a more spacious cabin

When you arrive, simply take your bags plane side and walk out to your waiting ride or grab a rental car from our on-site partners. No baggage claims, no crowds exiting, no annoying taxi lines.

The only downside is that travel is only offered in various California airports and Las Vegas.

I decided to test out a booking from Las Vegas to Orange County, California and I was pleasantly surprised with the rates. It only cost $118 total round trip! I am aware that rates flying within California or between Las Vegas and California airports may not be all that expensive but to be able to save time and eliminate the hustle and bustle of traditional commercial flights might be well worth the price.

"

I tend to run late for flights, so JetSuiteX is perfect.

I don't have to arrive an hour before my flight.

"

Photo Credit: JetSuiteX

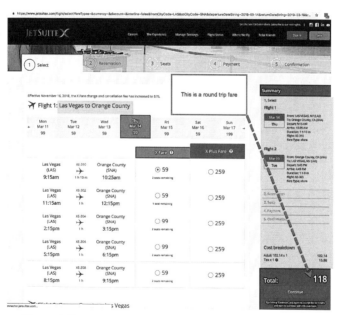

Business Travel Resources

Here are some of the recommended mobile apps and websites:

Hotel Tonight

I cannot tell you how many time I have had to use this on an emergency trip but this app has definitely come in handy. *Hotel Tonight* allows you to find last minute hotel deals even if a day or two out before your travel time. This especially comes in handy if you are headed to a conference and the host hotel is booked, you might find some great alternatives at great prices. Just search, select the best deal and book instantly.

TripIt

Okay, I must admit that *TripIt* has things laid out pretty well, especially tools for planning a trip. It allows you to plan and organize in the simplest way possible. From planning out your itinerary to storing your reservations and flight details, the great part about it is that your trip information is connected to your email account, so it pulls all your emails related to your trip and organizes the information effectively as well as it is easily accessible. The best option is to download the mobile app for greater convenience.

I like it because hours before my trip, a little notification alert would go off to let me know of my itinerary, flight details (going and coming), car rental, hotel information and any stops in between, keeping me on schedule. It will also send a notification if your plane is behind schedule. One of the new features for iPhone users is that you can create a Siri shortcut by giving it a voice tag like "Travel Plans". I am also able to add other email addresses of people who I'd like to have my schedule and know my whereabouts, especially for safety purposes.

There are additional features in the Pro version but if you don't choose to upgrade initially, you will still have access to some great features in their free plan. Another great option is that you can access your information from practically anywhere, mobile or desktop, so you will never have to worry about losing your schedule.

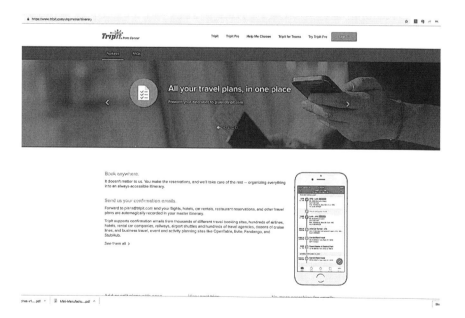

How to Save with using Google Flights

Google Flights has to be one of the best resources out there to book flights at the best price. The key to the best deals is to be flexible with your dates. Google Flights offers predictive pricing as well as suggested destinations. If you have a solid schedule, you can use this to compare the prices with airlines directly. Let's say that you live in Houston and have been planning to meet with a potential business partner, who resides in Los Angeles, in the next few months. You haven't really decided on a time frame and you also want to make sure that you are not spending excess on the trip.

In this example, this is for roundtrip fare from Houston to Los Angeles.

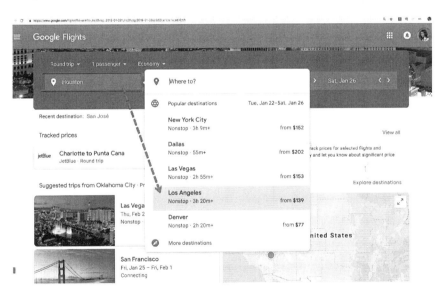

Once you select a city, the calendar will populate with potential pricing for trip cost for various days and you can scroll through the various months of the year in order to find the best prices. In this example below, we see that February has some great fares. The catch to this is not so much of the departure date as it is the return date because that is where your final fare will come from. We chose, Friday February 1st with a return date of February 4th with a RT cost of approximately $115. But wait, there's more...

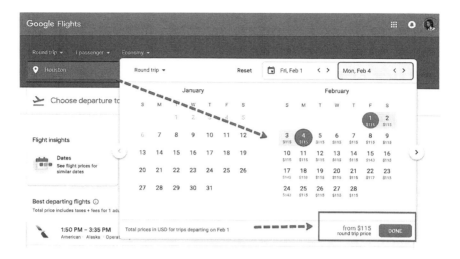

Here's some sample trips originating from Houston, Texas and entering a destination of "Asia".

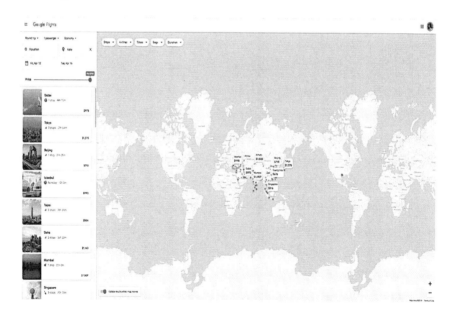

This search returned flights from Houston to Dubai for $973 RT, Tokoyo $1375 RT, Beijing $710 RT, Singapore $816 RT to name a few.

Google Flights has some additional tools, known as *Flight Insights* that will help you increase the chances of finding the best deals.

a. **Dates**

The dates feature shows you a matrix of similar dates and the flight prices for those dates. You can also us the advance filters to narrow your search results.

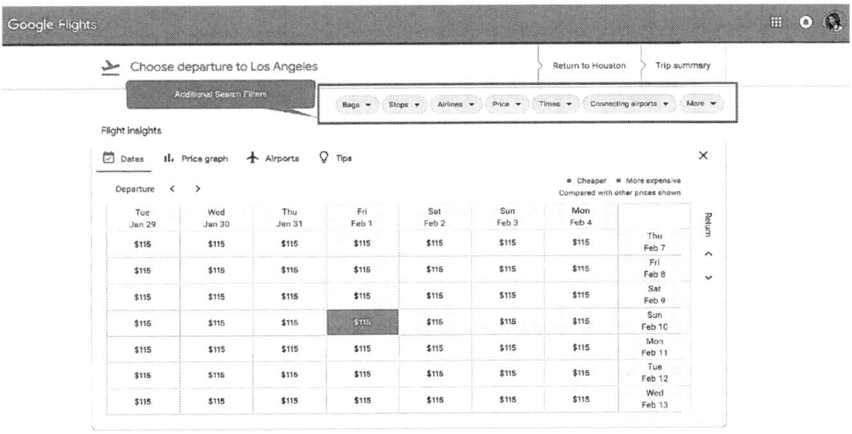

Google Flights

Choose departure to Los Angeles   Return to Houston   Trip summary

Additional Search Filters   Bags ▾   Stops ▾   Airlines ▾   Price ▾   Times ▾   Connecting airports ▾   More ▾

Flight insights

📅 Dates   �� ⅼ Price graph   ✈ Airports   ♀ Tips   ✕

Departure   ‹   ›   ● Cheaper   ■ More expensive — Compared with other prices shown

Tue Jan 29	Wed Jan 30	Thu Jan 31	Fri Feb 1	Sat Feb 2	Sun Feb 3	Mon Feb 4	
$115	$115	$115	$115	$115	$115	$115	Thu Feb 7
$115	$115	$115	$115	$115	$115	$115	Fri Feb 8
$115	$115	$115	$115	$115	$115	$115	Sat Feb 9
$115	$115	$115	$115	$115	$115	$115	Sun Feb 10
$115	$115	$115	$115	$115	$115	$115	Mon Feb 11
$115	$115	$115	$115	$115	$115	$115	Tue Feb 12
$115	$115	$115	$115	$115	$115	$115	Wed Feb 13

b. **Price Graph**

Out of all the features that *Google Flights* has to offer, I think the the Price Graph is my favorite. Maybe it's due to the fact the I love charts, diagrams, and infographics that displays data in different ways. The feature is pretty cool because you can look at the graph with the suggested date range and can immediately identify the dates that offers the lowest fares from ones with peak fares.

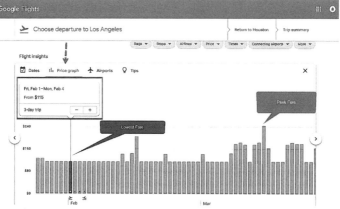

c. **Airports**

The airports option returns fares from the closest airports in range that you could fly out of. Some rules of thumbs for travel is to consider alternative airports to fly out of or in to, especially if the airport that you are using is not a major hub. Generally, when they are smaller airports the prices can be a little pricier or much lower than the main ones. However, depending on your schedule, you might just stick with flying out of the main airport to save you time and the struggle of trying to get to the alternative one.

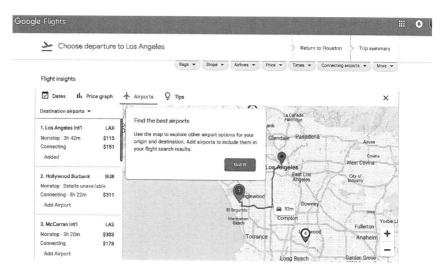

254

d. Tips

The tips feature is pretty interesting. It could give you tips to let you know when the best dates to fly out or if you are saving with the option you chose. It also suggests additional deals like adding hotel with your flight or any other resources that they have available and think that you would like to know about.

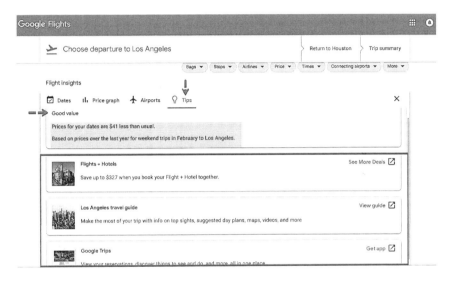

e. Tracking prices

Google Flights has an option that allows you to track prices. Since the service is connected to your Gmail account, it tracks your search queries and updates you via email if any of the prices change. I totally suggest that you enable this feature.

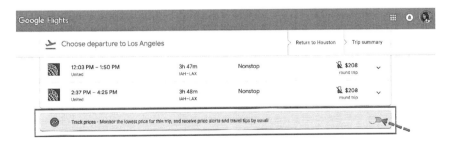

There are so many more features in options to explore with *Google Flights*, but I wanted to share the most important ones with you in order to get you started.

SkyScanner

SkyScanner is another one of my favorite apps that I've used for years. They've had quite of few updates since its inception. *Skyscanner* is a leading global travel search site, a place where people are inspired to plan and book direct from millions of travel options at the best prices. I decided to use the same search criteria that was used in *Google Flights* just to see if it would return comparable rates. So, let's just see...

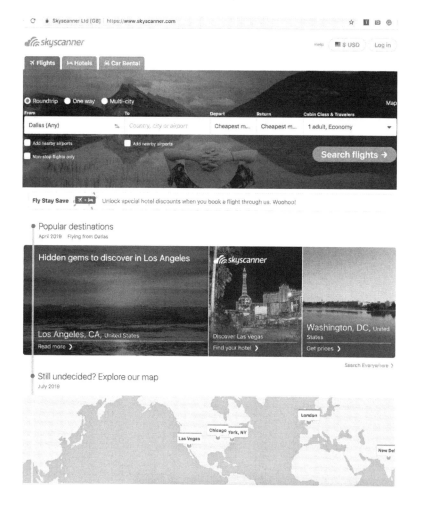

Before selecting on the what was available, Skyscanner prompted me to add a Price Alert, similar to the one in *Google Flights*.

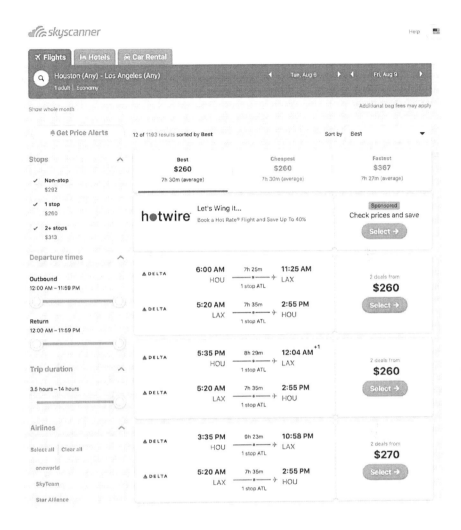

Before you make a final decision, make sure you check out their Daily Flight Deals. It could include your departure and destination.

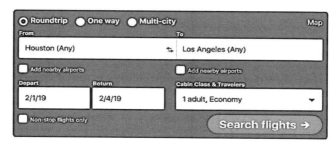

Looking for the best flight deals for your next trip? Find the top Skyscanner deals that are updated daily to book the cheapest flight up to 55% off the average price.

Start Your Flight Search Here

Top Daily Flight Deals

Departure City	Destination	Round-Trip Fare
Boston	San Juan	$202
Boston	Cancun	$269
Chicago	Toronto	$205
Chicago	London	$325
Los Angeles	Singapore	$426
Los Angeles	Bali	$533
Miami	Paris	$309
Miami	Barcelona	$294
New York City	Reykjavik	$230
New York City	Amsterdam	$317

These prices were valid as of January 6, 2019, and may not always be available. Bookmark this page — we'll be updating it daily!

Skyscanner also offers searches by *Whole Month or Cheapest Month.* All you need to do is enter your departure and arrival cities and select a month. So maybe you are hosting a huge conference (or attending one) and it is centered around the travel dates, as long as you are flexible then these options will definitely help cut expenses.

Whole Month:

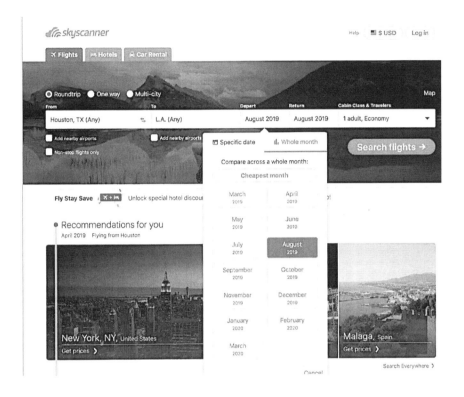

In this example, a RT flight from Houston to LA would be approximately $204.

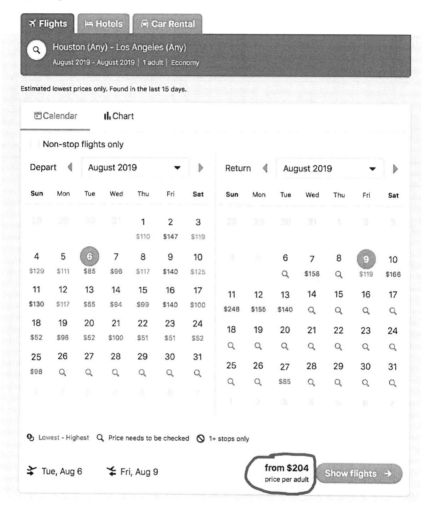

Cheapest Month:

The cheapest month to fly in this example was May, which returned a RT flight from Houston to Los Angeles for approximately $103.

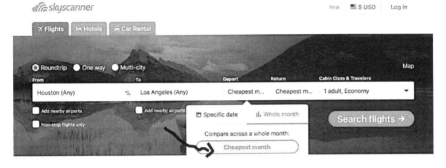

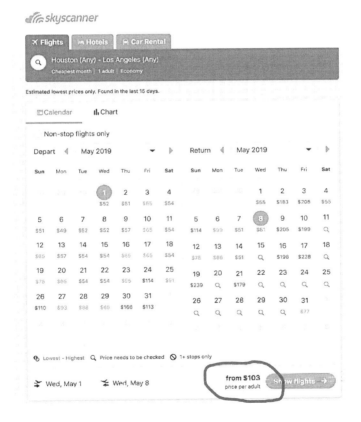

Airfare Watchdog

I can't go without referencing *Airfare Watchdog*. If your schedule permits flexibility, then check out their top daily deals from your home location. *Airfare Watchdog* will check multiple flight search engines to find the best rate. You can set a "watch" on the trip just before purchasing just in case prices change. On a personal note, I like the app better that searching via the website.

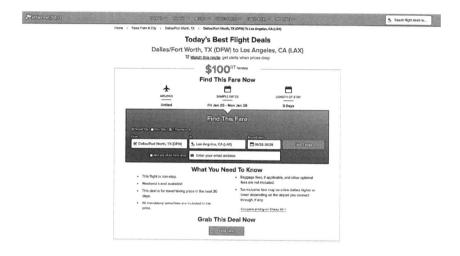

Additional Travel Resources for Business Travelers

Gate Guru

Gate Guru is a handy app that will help you track your flight and trip journey information as well as operating as a navigator while going through airport. It shows you the various airport amenities such as restaurants, shops, and services. This app may not necessarily save you money, but it can certainly help you in managing and saving for your trip.

Home

The Home screen serves as your base to navigate GateGuru as you like. The Home screen will display current and future journeys. For current journeys, as we receive data on your next departure, we populate that in an expanded state. The Home screen also gives you direct access to our AirportCard. The airport list is pre-populated based on closest airports, but you can also access any airport via the search bar.

Amenity List View

For users that add flights, much of the magic of GateGuru's day-of travel solution is behind the scenes, as we automatically connect the relevant parts of your day-of travel based on your flight information. So the amenity list view automatically shows information that is personalized to your trip – based on your departure or arrival terminal. If you want to see all of the amenities in the airport, just tap the terminal filter bottom in the bottom left.

263

LoungeBuddy - as mentioned earlier *LoungeBuddy* is a great app to have in your app library. The app is available for both iOS and Android.

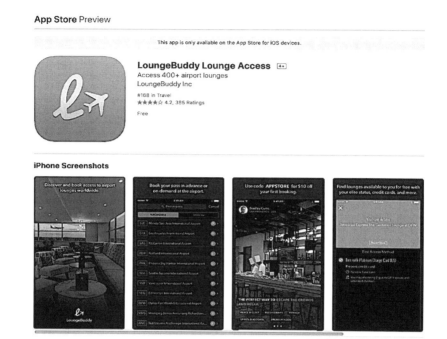

Recommended Book to Read: Business Travel Success: *How to Reduce Stress, Be More Productive & Travel with Confidence* by Carol Margolis

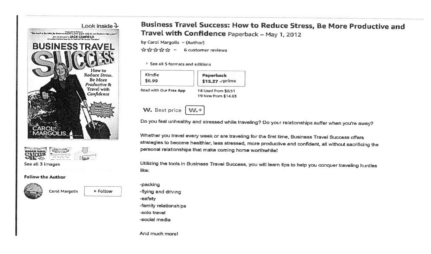

Acknowledgements

To every supporter: Thank you for inquiring, requesting, purchasing, sharing and reading this book...but more than that, I truly hope that something that you read inspires, motivates, or encourages you to live your best life, whether through travel or whatever you choose to do in life. Most of all, don't let anyone or anything hold you back from finishing what's in your heart to do. You may start out sprinting, then jogging, down to walking or you might even find yourself crawling to the finish line...but even if your knees are worn out from doing so, then roll over until you cross over.

There is a way.... whatever you do...Just Finish!

I returned, and saw under the sun, that the race is not to the swift, nor the battle to the strong, neither yet bread to the wise, nor yet riches to men of understanding, nor yet favour to men of skill; but time and chance happeneth to them all.
Ecclesiastes 9:11 KJV

Travel Agencies and Specialized Travel Groups

Golden Life Travel Agency "Living Life Like It's Golden"
Specializing in Cruise Parties across the Globe
Arleathia Chambliss - Owner/Travel Agent
Phone: (678) 362-2532
Facebook Page:
Facebook: Golden-Life-Travel-Agency

Cyntsational Travel
(Specializing in Group Travel/Cruise Parties)
Cynthia Hightower - Owner/Travel Agent
Phone: 706-593-0928
Email: cdhightower10@gmail.com
Facebook Page:
Facebook: Cyntsational-Travel

WCD Landseair Travel
(Specializing in Group Travel, Family/Class Reunions)
-The Queen of Group Travel-
Wanda Daniels - Owner/Travel Agent
Phone: (813) 784-0699
Website: www.wcdlandseairtravel.com
Facebook Page:
Facebook: WcdLandseairTravel/

220 Travel Group
(Specializing in Wine Crawls)
Glenn Murray
https://220communications.com/wine-crawl/wine-crawl/

Travel Quote

"What in the WORLD are you waiting on,
when the WORLD is waiting on YOU?"
- Brilliant Wanderer

Made in the USA
Columbia, SC
22 January 2023

10164827R00146